If rock music is causing a communications gap in your family, then *Rock and Roll* is the tool you need to build a bridge of understanding. In this updated new edition, J. Brent Bill examines the genre from a Christian perspective. This informative guide covers a number of topics, including:

- *rock and roll's history*
- *various styles*
- *current trends*
- *rock's continual appeal to young people*
- *the latest in contemporary Christian music*

In order to combat rock's harmful influences, Bill stresses the importance of families listening to music together and viewing lyrics in light of biblical principles. He also encourages parents, ministers, and youth leaders to look beyond the words to the message of the music. Because the message reveals the needs and concerns of young people today, you can learn how to reach them with the love of Christ. With its lighthearted yet biblical approach, *Rock and Roll* is a book family members can enjoy together.

BY J. Brent Bill

Rock and Roll
Stay Tuned
Lunch Is My Favorite Subject

ROCK *and* ROLL

J. BRENT BILL

Power Books

Fleming H. Revell Company
Old Tappan, New Jersey

Portions of this book, in different form, have appeared in *Group* magazine (Thom Schultz Publications, P.O. Box 481, Loveland, CO 80537) and are reprinted with their permission.

Acknowledgments for use of copyrighted material continue on page 160.

The Music Comparison Chart is Copyright ©1987 by Paul Baker, P.O. Box 508, Pinson, AL 35126. All rights reserved. Used by permission.
May not be duplicated without written permission from Paul Baker.
For information on obtaining poster-sized copies of the Music Comparison Chart write to Paul Baker, P.O. Box 508, Pinson, AL 35126.

Library of Congress Cataloging in Publication Data

Bill, J. Brent, date
  Rock and roll.

  "Power books."
  "Suggested reading list": p.
  1. Rock music—Religious aspects—Christianity.
I. Title.
ML3534.B55 1984   784.5'4   84-2125
ISBN 0-8007-5156-6

Contents

Acknowledgments

While one person's name may appear on the book jacket, I have discovered that it requires many good friends to produce a manuscript. These friends provide insight, helpful criticism, and much more that make a manuscript something worth reading and not just jumbles and heaps of words. The fine folks listed below were my partners on this project. Without their assistance, this book would never have appeared in print.

Two fine magazine editors, Jack Kirk and Gary Richardson, gave me my first opportunities for publication. Gary especially encouraged me to write about contemporary music. Their faith in my potential is greatly appreciated.

John and JoAnn Bill (also known as Dad and Mom) instilled in me two great loves—music and books. Their investment has culminated in this manuscript. For these loves, and for their love and support throughout my life and ministry, I am deeply grateful.

To my wife, Sharon, who put up with my stereo playing, long nights away while writing, and general neglect of everything from her to the yard while engaged in this project, thank you. Thanks for holding it all together for our family. I'll try to be home for dinner tomorrow night.

Many thanks also go to Paul Baker for his insight into CCM—especially as it expresses itself in the form of the "Sounds Like . . ." chart in the back of this book.

Finally, to Tom Mullen, to whom this epic is dedicated. Tom has been with me throughout the development of this book. It was he who first suggested I write it. He read each rewrite, making suggestions and criticisms that made it stronger. He shared my joy when it was accepted for publication. An excellent writer himself, he has helped me realize my dream of being published. At times like these, I realize how feeble words are when it comes to expressing the heart's desire. All I can really say is, Tom, I love you.

ROCK *and* ROLL

1
It's Only Rock and Roll

I like music. I'm also partial to silence—depending on the circumstances—but mostly I prefer music. I listen to it from the time I get up until I go to bed. When I move to a new house the first thing I do is hook up the stereo. While looking at cars I always check the radio. I can spend hours in record stores, browsing through the miles of bins, searching for just the right recording. I know many of you are just like me.

Usually I listen to rock. Other kinds of music are played at our house, though not as often. We play "beautiful" music during romantic, candle-lit dinners after our kids are fast asleep. Country and western makes an occasional appearance when the only rock we can get is what Sharon, my wife, calls "screaming" rock—Quiet Riot and the likes. We jump with jazz when we're feeling cool and show off our cultural class with Brahms and Beethoven. Most often, though, it's some form of rock echoing down our hallways. It might be the same at your house—depending on who owns the stereo and who pays the electric bill. Much of modern living is done in three-quarter time—with electric guitars, keyboards, bass, and drums lending expression and inspiration. It's there, real, and often fun.

There are two things that still nag at me about listening to rock: Mom and Dad. They had hoped that my tastes would become more refined and I would outgrow this silly desire to listen to rock (which my father still considers two levels below chimpanzees beating on tin cans and hooting). Alas, I still enjoy it. It's the music I grew up with. Though fascinated as a fifth grader by the Columbus (Ohio) Symphony's rendition of "Bugler's Holiday" (which I thought was "Burglar's Holiday"), the first song that really spoke to my spirit was a tune called "The Bristol Stomp." Soon after hearing that, my cousin Pete and some of his cronies started a rock-and-roll group. Known as the Fabulous Trends and acclaimed as much for their distinctive look (Pete was five-two and the tallest member was seven-two) as for their music, they made it onto the local charts with a rock ballad entitled "Class Ring." It is one of the few songs from that period of my life (the others being "The B-I-B-L-E" and "Sermon in Shoes") to which I can remember all of the words. They really stuck. This kinship with a real rock and roller kindled a flame that burns yet today.

I grew up with my generation and our rock groups. I knew which station was the hippest (the "new WCOL"), which songs the hottest, and which concerts the hugest. I grew up singing along with the Beach Boys, Jan and Dean, the Beatles, the Hollies, the Association, and a host of others. I taught myself how to play guitar and played in a few groups. Other musical interests were encouraged by my mother (jazz) and father (light classics), but when I wanted *real* music, it was rock-and-roll time. It was our music, the music of youth. Through it all, I remained a good Christian kid, involved in church activities and youth fellowship.

Why say all this? Because I am not unique—at least so far as my taste in music. Scores of people like rock and roll. Why else would it be a multibillion-dollar-a-year business? In the early 1980s Americans were spending over $1.5 billion a year on recorded rock. That's just records and tapes. Add in the figures for rock magazines, concerts, posters, T-shirts, and all other rock-related paraphernalia and the amount is staggering. Bruce Springsteen's *Born in the USA* tour took in over $100 million. And that is just in the United States. We all know that people buy what they like. They obviously like rock. The hard part for the Christian comes in where faith and rock meet.

As I've said, I was a Christian teenager. If my birth certificate didn't tell me otherwise, I would think I had been born in church. I know I grew up there. Attendance was a given at Sunday school and morning worship. And unless Grandma Fortune flew in from California (like she did every three years or so and got me off the hook), there was Sunday evening worship, youth fellowship, and midweek prayer meeting. If there was a service, I was there. I went because Mom and Dad made me, but I also went because I felt a responsibility to spiritual growth. I knew just going to church wouldn't turn me into a Christian any more than sleeping in a garage would make me a Corvette. I had a relationship with Christ, the Living Lord of the universe. I wanted my life to show it. So I went to church and rallies. I believed that my being a Christian meant having standards that went against those of the world. Today I am a Christian minister and I still believe that.

Being a faithful attender of church camps and rallies, I frequently heard about the evil influence of rock and roll. Most speakers, who were older and wiser (?), expressed concern over the spiritual well-being of anyone who listened to rock. They made it seem as though rock was the root of all evil. This *music* was the cause of the moral decay of the "American way of life." Lack of respect for elders, juvenile delinquency, drug use, and illicit sex were all a result of rock's influence on its listeners.

Certainly if this were true—and we were morally prohibited from questioning the speaker's veracity—good Christians like ourselves would have nothing to do with this sort of sordid singing. I felt guilty. So did many of my friends. After all, we liked the stuff. We learned the new songs. We played our records until they wore out (they "wore out" much to our parents' delight). Were we then unfit to enter the Kingdom of Heaven? Were rock and rollers to be lumped together with fornicators, idolaters, adulterers, and other horrible types? It seemed so. "The choice is clear," thundered the mighty voices, "either God or rock, saints or sinners, Heaven or hell." That was easy for the thundering voices. They neither liked nor understood rock. We did. Though we pledged our allegiance to Christ and His church, we liked to sing "Amazing Grace" to the tune of "House of the Rising Sun." Worse yet, we liked "House of the Rising Sun" even without the lyrics of "Amazing Grace." We continued to listen to rock. We continued to feel guilty about it. We occasionally felt doomed.

I don't anymore. I have matured enough emotionally and spiritually to realize that many of the speakers were addressing the subject merely out of their own biases. They didn't like it and found it threatening. Since kids chose it over "good" music, there had to be something evil about the way it seduced them into listening. So they preached against it.

I would like to say that this type of uninformed preaching which lays needless guilt on good kids has ended—but it hasn't. It still goes on. In clammy church basements and steamy summer camps, speakers continue to decry the woeful debasement by demon Rock. An example is a former high school classmate of mine.

This friend, whom (to protect the innocent—me) we'll call John Doe (original, isn't it), and I went to the same schools from junior high on. We sat next to each other in homeroom our last two years of high school. John and I talked about the things that guys in our day talked about—cars, girls, cars, sports, cars, food, and cars. We also talked about which songs we liked and why (usually, "has a good beat"). Then came a sweltering June day in 1969. With thousands of parents and relatives crammed into Magley Stadium, our alma mater wafting on the breeze ("As toward the West the constant sun proceeds . . ."), we stumbled, blinded by the flashcubes atop Instamatics, to receive our diplomas. Friends who seemed such an integral part of our lives quietly faded with the onslaught of summer and then college in the fall. John was one of those who faded. I never saw him again. But I have heard him.

A few years ago Kathleen, one of my sisters, called. She said that she and Paul, her husband, had heard that John was going to be giving a series of lectures on rock and roll. Since they were held at a local church that Kathleen and Paul were familiar with, they went and tape-recorded the series. Then they sent the tapes to me, thinking it would be nice for two high school chums to have some contact. I appreciated that—at first. Later, I wasn't so sure.

As the tapes rolled through the recorder, it became clear that he wasn't lecturing on rock, he was preachin' agin it. With the force and fervor of a sawdust-trail evangelist, he told how rock and roll was much more than the vast moral wasteland I had always thought it to be. It had become an actual tool of the devil. Lucifer himself was in control of rock and roll and was out to destroy the Christian American Heritage granted us by our God-fearin' forefathers. Satan had his slimy mitts on the rock bands. While unsuspecting youths played records by a group called KISS, they were being unconsciously seduced by the *Knights In Satanic Service*. And KISS was not the only such group—how about Santana? Drop the first *n* and the last *a* and what have you got? Together now—SATAN! He told how rock and rollers gathered around record-pressing machines, laying their hands on the vinyl, dedicating the records to Satan, that his evil power might destroy the morals of America's youth.

According to my former classmate, this perversion named rock had begun its insidious work. Statistics showed that most teenage pregnancies resulted from sexual activity stimulated by rock and roll. Rock was the reason behind the rise in juvenile delinquency. It led to drinking, drugs, and dancing. Shame and scandal. What was a good Christian kid to do? Why, turn that vile vinyl over to John Doe for direct disposal. Get that smutty stuff out of your house—and over to his. When I finally quit laughing at his ignorant performance, I was ready to cry—for all the kids who had been taken in and made to feel terrible because they liked music played on electric guitars. I was sad because he had lied. His presentation was a gimmick, a cheap shot to press his point. The truth of what he said—that many rock lyrics are rotten, as are the musicians' life-styles—was negated by how he said it. A lack of facts and a lot of fiction and bombast were his mainstay. The kids felt guilty, but for things that weren't even true.

John couldn't tell you where his statistics on teenage pregnancy, drinking, and drugs came from. He had read them "somewhere." Never mind that KISS said they picked their name to remind people of a kiss or that Santana is merely the last name of the bandleader, Carlos Santana. It was of no concern that records come off a press so fast you couldn't pray over them if you wanted to, and that if you did happen to grab a piece of molten vinyl you would flame-broil your fingers, ruin the record, and alienate the accountant all in one move. Rock and roll is evil. So, from John's point of view, facts are to be used, misused, or ignored in his quest for demon Rock. After all, he's on a mission from God. Or so he claims.

Lest I seem too hard on John, let me say that he is not the only religious reviler of rock. There are many. Some are better, some worse. Some use the printing press as their method of reaching people with the message; others still preach and lead seminars. There are those who are serious and concerned; others are out to make a name for themselves.

Bob Larson is, perhaps, the best-known religious rock critic. He is the author of numerous books and articles about (read *against*) rock. According to his book *Rock*, the music kids listen to is responsible for sexual behavior, drug use, involvement in the occult, and interest in Eastern religion. This all happens because records are in the home. Larson quotes one teen as saying, "My music was gradually brainwashing me until I almost quit serving the Lord completely."[1]

This sort of scrambled thinking shifts moral responsibility from a living, breathing person to an inanimate hunk of plastic. Instead of, "the devil made me do it," it's now, "the record made me do it."

As a result of their lectures called, "What the Devil's Wrong With Rock Music?" the Peters brothers of Zion Christian Center estimate that $2 million worth of records and tapes have been destroyed. The brothers claim that "rock music is the largest Satanic force in America."[2]

Every town seems to have its religious rock-hater. From ascribing mysterious evil power to the beat, to warning of the dangers of alleged "backward masking," they go forth spreading gospels of guilt and fear, all the while ignoring the need to proclaim God's goodness and grace. They would rather dwell on the sordid than the spiritual.

Anyone who has ever looked at rock closely will agree that many rock lyrics are sinful and that some musicians' lives are far from Christian. On that we all can agree. It has been referred to as "raunch and roll"—and oftentimes rightfully so. Much of it is unwholesome.

The guilt trips laid on young believers are likewise unwholesome. Radios roost silently atop dressers. Turntables don't turn. Records and tapes are incinerated or given away. But for how long? Some kids will have the fortitude the preachers require of them and never listen again; most won't. A few miles into the trip home from camp or youth group the car radio will be blasting out Top 40 hits. That's because rock has become as much a part of our culture as *TV Guide*, Levi's, and the Golden Arches.

All of the above are the reasons for this book. It will be a chance to look at rock from a Christian perspective. I admit that I like rock—most of it anyway. The important thing is to learn how to see what the music's saying and not just react to it.

It's time for honesty. If you like all rock regardless, you won't like some of the things the book says. If you think it's all of the devil, you won't like it at all. If you are trying to understand, cope, live with, or enjoy rock sensibly, this is the book for you. We'll look at its history, messages (hidden and open), selective listening, toleration (for parents), and the Solid Rock. Have fun with the book and keep an open mind. Sit back and relax—it's only rock and roll.

---

1. Bob Larson, *Rock: Practical Help for Those Who Listen to the Words and Don't Like What They Hear* (Wheaton: Tyndale House Publishers, 1980), p. 86.

2. "Rock Report, Part 1," *Contemporary Christian Music* (August–September 1981), p. 15.

2
Rock Roots

By the time I reached _____'s concert on
Tuesday last week, the opening number was
over, the audience in bold enthusiasm, and the
piano a wreck. Regarded as an immensely
spirited young harmonious blacksmith, who
puts a song on the piano as upon an anvil, and
hammers it out with an exuberant enjoyment of
the swing and strength of the proceeding,
_____ is at least exhilarating; and his
hammer play is not without variety . . . but his
touch, light or heavy, is the touch that hurts; and
the glory of his playing is the glory that attends
murder. . . . Besides, the piano is not an
instrument upon which you can safely let
yourself go in this fashion.[1]

A review of Billy Joel pounding out "Modern Woman" at
the Philadelphia Spectrum? Perhaps Elton John "Crocodile
Rock"-ing at Madison Square Garden in the seventies? How
about Jerry Lee Lewis grinding out "Great Balls of Fire" in
the fifties? Afraid not. This review is from the nineties—the
1890s! The reviewer is playwright George Bernard Shaw,

and the concert took place in London in 1890. The pianist's name was Paderewski, and you can be sure he had never heard of rock and roll.

Ignace Jan Paderewski, the man whose "piano was a wreck," is known as a pianist, composer, and statesman. Far from being a bullyboy on the piano, he is perhaps Poland's best-known classical composer, whose most important works include Symphony in B Minor and the opera *Manru*. The chief sources of his concert repertoire were Bach, Beethoven, Schumann, and Chopin. He was hailed for his musical mastery of the classics, his intellect, and his virtuosity. Paderewski was one of the most highly regarded pianists of his age. He was a true star in the musical sky. Yet Shaw, also intellectual and cultured, had little use for him.

A fun story, you say, but what is the point? The point is—taste is purely subjective. Throughout musical history, new forms and innovations have not always gained immediate acceptance. People get used to hearing music done a certain way and think that thereafter *that* is how music has to be. Certainly Paderewski and his distinctive styling didn't receive instant acclaim from all listeners. Yet, as time went by, he was honored for his achievements and seen for what he was—a truly great musician. He was even made director of the Warsaw Conservatory. It just took time for people to get used to him and recognize his talents.

The acceptance of an entire type, as opposed to just one person, sometimes takes a while as well. The approval of some forms, especially of popular music, comes quickly. Examples would be the mellow sounds of easy listening and folk music. Some have to wait longer. Jazz and country-western both carried cultural stigma that made their widespread acceptance slow in coming. After a period of time, though, most forms are granted a place in the musical world. Rock is still searching for its place, for generally it has gone unrecognized as a legitimate form of music. Since it is geared toward the youth market, it is regarded as less serious than other types of music. But as we look at rock, we can see that it deserves to be considered as much more than music by mindless guitar-playing morons.

Music has a history that is long and varied. It begins with our ancestors' first song and stretches to the complexity of the modern symphony. The civilizations of the past each produced unique styles. We who hold the Bible dear have many examples of songs that were important to the people of faith. From Deborah's Song in Judges 5, to the majesty and grandeur of the wide-ranging Psalms, we see the value the Israelites placed on musical expression. The early Christians used hymns as teaching devices. Music is still an important item for the worshiping community.

Secular music has also come a long way from our forebears pounding out rhythms on primitive drums. Pythagoras, the Greek mathematician, pondered the musical notes produced by strings of various lengths. The Middle Ages produced the wandering minstrels with their folk songs. The symphony was powerfully molded by Beethoven, and redirected and defined by his twentieth-century counterparts—with each one's nationality greatly contributing to his unique style. Opera, of course, was also introduced and accepted as a musical form of worth.

At the same time, paralleling serious music, popular forms were developing. Thus we had comic or light operas and the light classics. The fact that music was a part of common life is illustrated by the tune Martin Luther chose for "A Mighty Fortress Is Our God." Though it now sounds rather dignified and refined when sung by Sunday morning congregations, it was originally a rousing drinking tune in German beer gardens. Luther picked it because he wanted a song that the people already knew. It helped bring the gospel to life.

Popular music, the music of the masses, also changes rapidly, much more quickly than symphonic styles. That is because it reflects the mood of society. In the days when the United States entered the fray of World War I, the songs extolled the glories of "Pershing's Crusaders" and proclaimed, "America, Here's My Boy." Lest we think that protest songs are something relatively new, another song from that time declared, "I Didn't Raise My Boy to Be a Soldier." As the Great Depression filled the skies with its impenetrable clouds of economic despair, many folks identified with those singing, "Brother, Can You Spare a Dime." Others who, though financially strapped also, had a more optimistic attitude, looked skyward for "Pennies From Heaven." Americans have had songs about every stage of our national life. Some have been popular songs, some blues numbers, others of a country-western bent, and yet others were rock and roll. The antiwar songs of the Top 40 in the sixties and seventies by Bob Dylan, Country Joe and the Fish, and others, are still fresh in the minds of many Americans. As noted, rock, like other forms of popular music, is a reflection of the times. To understand it as just one of America's many musical styles, and not some diabolic device of the devil, means we need to look at its roots. Its parents are respectable members of the popular music scene.

Rock roots lie deep in rhythm and blues and country-western. In the early fifties both forms lay outside the mainstream of popular music. Rhythm and blues (R & B) and country and western (C & W) were beamed via radio to minority audiences. R & B, known as "race" music at that time, was played to a large, mostly urban, black audience in the major markets of New York and Philadelphia, with a few other urban areas thrown in. C & W meanwhile was played for rural, white listeners, mostly living in the Southeast extending to Texas. Neither form was listened to by very many people in other areas. That's the way it remained until rock came along. Rock developed as a hybrid of the two, and though others played it, the first to propagate this new style in a big way was a group known as Bill Haley and the Comets. The year was 1953. The song was "Crazy, Man, Crazy."

Bill Haley got his start in C & W, playing dollar-a-night dance gigs in the Midwest. Neither his career nor his band were meteoric at that time. The band was called the Saddlemen. On a venture close to a big city, Haley was exposed to R & B and decided to liven up his dance sets by interjecting a blend of R & B and C & W. The dancers loved it, so he recorded some of his numbers. "Crazy, Man, Crazy" hit the charts, and rock and roll began to get national exposure. Other people pioneered the way for Haley, but it was he and his renamed Saddlemen who brought it to America's attention. With the screening of the film *The Blackboard Jungle*, the band that sang the movie's theme song was launched into orbit. The biggest song in America was Bill Haley and the Comets' "Rock Around the Clock."

In addition to "Crazy, Man, Crazy," 1953 saw another important development in rock. Disc jockey Alan Freed of WJW in Cleveland began playing R & B on his late-night show, "Moondog's Rock and Roll Party." The show was aimed at a white, middle-class teen audience, and it was a big success. His first live show had over thirty thousand teens trying to get a seat. The fear that a white audience wouldn't stand for R & B, though acute, was proved false. Freed's success with this new type of programming he called rock and roll made him highly sought after. Finally he left Cleveland for New York and WINS, there to introduce Big Apple-ites to the joys of rock.

In spite of promising beginnings, rock fever spread slowly. At first, it was largely regional like its forebears. There was no "American Top 40" with Casey Kasem or "American Bandstand" hosted by Dick Clark. It took the appearance in 1955 of *Blackboard Jungle* and two new stars—Chuck Berry and Elvis Presley—to boost rock into money-making, popular status.

Chuck Berry came from the roots of rock—he was black, and he knew and loved R & B. He, maybe more than most, saw the huge commercial potential of a mass market; so he structured his songs and performances to it. Because of such shrewd insight, his songs "Johnny B. Goode," "You Never Can Tell," "Sweet Little Sixteen," and many others gained acceptance by white teenagers, making him the first black ever to register consistent approval. Though perhaps less famous than Presley, his style and songs influenced rock at least as much—if not more. Many later groups—the Beatles, the Rolling Stones, Gerry and the Pacemakers are examples—used Berry's material as hit vehicles. His greatest strength is his appeal to different audiences. His stage presence is riveting, his shows electric. He personifies the word *entertainer.*

The Elvis Presley story is better known, especially since his tragic death in 1977. A Memphis truck driver, Presley cut some records at Sam Phillips's Sun Recording Studio. While they were only moderate successes at first, they provided him a base for touring the South, playing his own unique blend of C & W and R & B. His manager, Colonel Tom Parker, knew a good thing when he had one and urged the sultry singer to put more emphasis on the R & B. The move was the right one, to say the least. RCA Records became aware of Presley's southern success, saw the potential, and purchased his contract and early recordings for $35,000 and a new Cadillac for Elvis. It was money well spent. With songs like "Heartbreak Hotel," "Hound Dog," and "Jailhouse Rock," Presley became a national star and a gold mine for RCA. In his first two years with RCA he gave them the number-one slot on the singles chart for fifty-five weeks.

The King, as he came to be known, was rock's first true superstar. He reigned triumphantly on records and television (many still remember his "Ed Sullivan Show" appearance). He also became a movie star. His first film, *Love Me Tender* in 1956, was pure fluff; but it established Presley as a box-office draw. Presley starred in over thirty films, often coupled with the biggest stars of the day. His career soared until his induction into the army—and then it skyrocketed. The whole rock-and-roll world snapped up any Presleyana that Colonel Parker allowed out. People expected great things when he was released from the service, but they were disappointed. His postarmy music didn't live up to expectations. Gone was much of the verve and vitality of the early Elvis. He seemed unable to recapture the drama or presence he possessed in the fifties. His influence on rock waned. The late sixties saw him once again take a stab at greatness, with "In the Ghetto" and "Suspicious Minds." Such songs, though, were conspicuous because of their infrequency.

But while Elvis's popularity faded on the radio, it blossomed in Vegas. Astute management on the part of Parker transformed Presley into Mr. Showman. His Las Vegas acts and road shows were constant sellouts. Toward the end, though, his grasp on his once-loyal subjects weakened. In August 1977, grossly overweight and hooked on pills, Presley died. The King had fallen from his throne.

Presley's influence on rock can hardly be overestimated. He, and the ever-present Colonel Tom Parker, took a type of music that had little national exposure and parlayed it into commercial greatness and big business. His ties to RCA took rock from its early days of independent labels to major studio releases. Other recording companies wanted a piece of the action being generated by this musical maniac from Memphis. His appearances on the Dorsey Brothers, Steve Allen, and Ed Sullivan shows gave evidence of the fame that could be obtained through wise use of that young medium. *King Creole* and the other Presley films showed that rock-and-roll stars were money-makers in the movies. Elvis Presley souvenirs ("I Love Elvis" and "I Hate Elvis" buttons were both shrewdly marketed by Parker) paved the way for today's marketing of T-shirts, tour jackets, belt buckles, and the like in record and clothing stores. Dollar-a-night dance sets have given way to $200,000, standing-room-only concerts in the world's largest arenas. All because of Elvis.

What was more important than commercial influence, at least as far as the young listeners were concerned, was Presley's rebellious blend of C & W and R & B. The formula first broadcast nationally by Haley was transformed by Presley. Haley's material paled next to Presley's raw-edged rock. Besides, Presley was young like the listeners, while Haley was an old man of thirty-three when he hit the charts. Presley paved the way for innovative rock in the early years. His throbbing prearmy recordings are among the best rock ever. They were driving, exciting, and alive. He was the cornerstone for all that was to come. As Buddy Holly said, "Without Elvis, none of us could have made it."[2]

Though largely based on R & B, very little fifties rock was popularized by black artists. Chuck Berry, already mentioned, is the most notable exception. Songs by black singers or groups might make it onto the charts, but only if a white group "covered," or rerecorded, them. Rarely did a black composition make it in its original recorded form. "Sh-Boom" is an example. Recorded as a R & B tune by a black group called the Cords, "Sh-Boom" sold big, went on the R & B charts, and eventually made it, for a brief time, to the national pop chart. But while many people today remember the song, it's not the Cords' version they recall. The arrangement that everyone knows was a cover by the Crew Cuts. With a name like that you'd probably guess they were white. And you'd be right. The Crew Cuts' "Sh-Boom" was released the same week that the Cords' version went on the charts, and reached the Top 10 in just one week. The song even appeared on the C & W charts when it was covered by Bobby Williamson. "Sh-Boom" is just one example of how a black tune had to be covered to make it in a white listening audience.

The careers of Pat Boone and other stars of that time rested heavily on the writing of black groups. While the music was gaining popularity, its black originators weren't. White listeners liked R & B, as long as it was performed by white groups. Even early innovators realized that. When Alan Freed started "Moondog's Rock and Roll Party," he called it that because he was sure that people would be turned off by the racial overtones of a "Rhythm and Blues Party." Fats Domino, Chubby Checker, the Cords, the Drifters, and other black groups were relegated to nonstarring roles in the larger-than-life version of early rock. They were essential to rock's development, yet were almost totally ignored by the white listeners. As people today research the roots of rock, these long-disregarded artists are getting the recognition they deserve.

To list all the stars and hit-makers of the fifties would be impossible. They include Buddy Holly, Little Richard, Jerry Lee Lewis, Sam Cooke, the Everly Brothers, and Dick Clark and his "American Bandstand." While the style varied from group to group, in many ways it was the same—animated, up-to-date, and crazy, man, crazy.

Scandal broke in 1959 and 1960. The United States House of Representatives' Special Committee on Legislative Oversight began an investigation of *payola*. Put simply, payola is paying for playing. The record companies would give deejays money and other enticements to make sure that their records got airplay. Lots of airplay made a song a hit, and a hit meant lots of records purchased by the teens. Though many folks in the know contended that this practice had existed since the beginnings of recorded music and radio, rock and roll was a fast-growing and hated (by many adults) industry. Thus it was particularly vulnerable. The investigation purported to be about the illegal hyping of recorded product, but centered largely around the investigators' disdain for this new form of music. Two of the main witnesses were Alan Freed and Dick Clark. Clark's dialogues with Representative Steve Derounian were often humorous. They also reveal, however, the contempt with which rock was held by these responsible national leaders. The entire proceedings are in a 1,600-page document entitled "Responsibilities of Broadcasting Licenses and Station Personnel." Though there is evidence that some payola still exists, the hearings had their effect. Alan Freed, unsophisticated champion of rock and R & B, was ruined. Dick Clark, the clean-cut, all-American announcer, and his Philadelphia white sound, went on to greater success than could be imagined. Rock itself became less rowdy in its beat and melody than it had been in the fifties. Though still not the choice of thinking adults, it had been changed to a degree that made it much less offensive. This savage had been sanitized.

The sixties sailed in with slick promotion and big new sounds. Gone were the rockabilly of Buddy Holly and the gyrations of Elvis. Instead there was the California sound—surfing music by the Beach Boys. The Beach Boys were originally known as Carl and the Passions, comprised of Brian, Carl, and Dennis Wilson, Mike Love, and Al Jardine. They switched from plain old rock and roll to surfing music after being persuaded to do so by Dennis. Their first record, recorded in 1961 on the Candix label, was called "Surfin'" and reached number seventy-six on the national Hot 100. Candix, a small, independent company, assumed they were a one-song phenomenon and promptly folded. The Wilsons' father, Murray, was convinced that his boys had potential. He took some of their recorded tracks to various companies, but no one was interested. Finally, Capitol

Records decided to take a chance. They purchased the masters for three hundred dollars. In June 1962, they released "Surfin' Safari" as a single. It shot to the top. Surf music became a national craze, and the Beach Boys were riding the ultimate wave.

The Beach Boys, Jan and Dean, and other Southern Cal clones infected the rest of America with beach-blanket fever. The songs were "Fun, Fun, Fun," "California Girls," "Be True to Your School," "Deadman's Curve," "Good Vibrations," and other tributes to eternal youth under the bright California sun. Though many of these groups were to wither under the onslaught of the British invasion in the mid-sixties, the Beach Boys endured. They constantly worked with new material, but kept the sound distinctly Beach Boys. Their music, just right for the early sixties, remained right because of their versatility. While most closely identified with surf and sun in the sixties, they are still a potent force in pop music. They consistently draw huge crowds for concerts and make the charts. The Beach Boys have endured. Though the 1983 drowning of Dennis Wilson slowed them down for a while, they're coming back around. Don't ever count them out.

Other stars from the early sixties were Gene Pitney, Bobby Rydell, Ricky Nelson, the Four Seasons, and—Dick Clark and his "American Bandstand." Another type of music that was gaining popularity among young listeners was folk music. Foremost among these artists were the Kingston Trio; Peter, Paul, and Mary; and the Chad Mitchell Trio (which was to include at one time an aspiring entertainer named John Denver). In many ways, songs like "Puff the Magic Dragon," "Tom Dooley," and "Blowin' in the Wind" bridged the gap between young and old. Though the music was lively, the discs rotated at 33⅓ instead of 45. This fact alone eased many adult minds. Even Mitch Miller, who loathed rock and roll, issued an album of folk song sing-alongs. Folk was never to replace rock, even as mellow as rock had become; but the days of sock-hop rock were numbered.

Paul Revere had been born two hundred years too early. Though he roused sleeping colonists in the late eighteenth century, the only successful British invasion didn't come until 1964. That was the year that four mop-topped Liverpudlians descended onto the United States with an "Ed Sullivan Show" appearance and the songs "I Want to Hold Your Hand" and "She Loves You." Their weapons were electric guitars, a bass guitar, and drums, all played to a plain and simple beat, the beat of fifties rock which was long forgotten by American rockers. The group's name was a combination of their style of music and a memorial. They wanted people to know they played "beat" music and they also wanted to honor a group that had influenced them, Buddy Holly and the Crickets. So they took an insect name like their heroes and fused it with the beat: Beetles + beat = the Beatles. And the Beatles = millions of dollars. They were only the first of the foreign fauna to land. The Animals, Herman's Hermits, the Zombies, and the Yardbirds all followed and scored big. But the Beatles were here first and it was the Beatles who changed the face of rock.

Like their counterpart of the fifties—Elvis—the Beatles all came from humble origins. Also like him, they enjoyed moderate success in the beginning. And for a final comparison, they were discovered by a manager who dreamed big dreams. His name was Brian Epstein.

Epstein first saw the Beatles in 1961, playing in a local pub in Liverpool. One of the steady groups at The Cavern, the band was comprised of John Lennon, Paul McCartney, George Harrison, and Pete Best. Best, a drummer, was fired by the rest of the group and replaced, in 1962, by Richard Starkey, who came to be better known as Ringo Starr. Epstein carefully groomed and managed the four through their early years.

The Beatles turned out to be much more than good—they were great. Their music recaptured the fire and drive of rock's early years. Beatlemania swept the United States and shot them to the top of the world's music scene. As Presley flew in the fifties, so the Beatles soared in the sixties. Every song they released not only made the charts, but dominated them. They still lead the list of artists with the most number-one hits. They hold twenty to Elvis's eighteen. The crown of rock was passed reluctantly from Memphis to Liverpool.

The Beatles have been much discussed. The subject of numerous books (the best being *Shout!* by Philip Norman), magazine articles, and radio and television interviews, they were larger than life—made so by their fans. Whenever a Beatle made a statement, it was received as if it were some ultimate truth or demonic utterance, not merely a passing remark by an entertainer. John Lennon's famous—or infamous, depending on your point of view—statement that the Beatles were "more popular than Jesus" is a case in point. This observation, which unfortunately was true, was taken as evidence of the group's anti-Christian stance. Others perceived it as a philosophical statement. This comment and many that followed turned the Beatles into spokesmen for any and all causes. They were seen as more than musicians; somehow they became messiahs for a confused generation.

They were musicians, and as such they were good; but as messiahs, they failed. As they and their world changed, so did their music. They were not content to rest on past glories, they stayed on the cutting edge of rock and roll. But they began to crumble. They got into drugs and Eastern mysticism for a while. Their marriages fell apart. It became apparent that the dispensers of truth were as confused as the rest of the world. All the power and glory that was theirs may well have led to their 1970 breakup. In the end they were less artists and more wealthy, unskilled businessmen and gurus with no real answers.

From the Beatles, though, came some of today's finest songs—"Yesterday," "Penny Lane," "When I'm Sixty-Four," "Something," and more. Unlike Elvis, who was chiefly an interpreter of other people's songs, the Beatles wrote their own music. Paul McCartney and John Lennon made up one of the most prolific song-writing teams ever. Except for John Lennon, who was gunned down in 1980, the Beatles are still contributing individually to rock music. They have never had the impact they had when they were the Beatles, but neither has anyone who followed them. Their music does reflect a mellowing and maturing of these renegade radicals who ruled the American airwaves. They once changed the times, now time has changed them.

The only common link among all the British groups was their Britishness. Peter and Gordon, Herman's Hermits, and the Rolling Stones were as different from one another as Frank Sinatra and Rudy Vallee. America, the birthplace of rock, had a sudden infatuation with anything British. From cute little MGs and Triumphs, to clothes from Carnaby Street, anything with a Union Jack on it sold. Especially music. In order to compete, American groups had to recapture some of the past that had given the English groups their inspiration. Suddenly everybody had Beatle haircuts and was singing imitations of "Love Me Do." American "British" groups like the Monkees (a group formed to make a hit TV show) were usually commercially successful. The Monkees sold in excess of 20 million records, even though they were the bane of the critics. The British Invasion went from 1964 to late 1968. Then heavy metal fell from the sky.

The late sixties and early seventies saw the advent of a form that is rightly called "hard rock." Hard rock grew out of "acid rock," a San Franciscan development of the hippie drug experience. It relied heavily on Indian *raga* forms and the use of instruments like the sitar. When the music gained national exposure it became less acid and more hard. The sound was driving and abrasive, and an assault on the listener's senses. It fit well with the drug scene, where people's senses were already scrambled. Among the best-known of these groups were the Doors, whose leader, Jim Morrison, strange even in the best of times, was the son of a navy admiral. Also superstars in this genre were Janis Joplin and Jimi Hendrix, though Joplin's tunes leaned more toward the blues side than straight out heavy metal. Joplin, Hendrix, and Morrison all died drug-related deaths, lonely at the top. The groups they were in, plus Steppenwolf and Jefferson Airplane, helped FM radio's new prestige. Hard-rock songs were too long and loud for commercial-oriented AM stations. FM was known as a purveyor of supermarket, or easy-listening, music. When the first FM "album" rock stations appeared, an FM receiver came to be a symbol of a progressive mind, a victory over the triviality of Top 40. With death, came rebirth. When Hendrix et al. passed from the scene, so did most of "drug" rock. People, artists and listeners alike, realized that they were playing with death and backed off. Many performers using drugs to keep ahead in the grueling world of touring and recording dropped out until they could come back "clean." The groups that followed were loud, but they played music of life, not death.

The Chi-Lites, Sly and the Family Stone, Chicago, the Guess Who, and others ushered in the seventies. The sound moved mostly from harshness to harmony. The driving beat was still there, but redirected. It was once again music to sing along with or dance to. It was good old rock and roll.

Unlike past periods, there was no domination by a certain sound. Rock was too wide now to be dominated by rockabilly, surfing, English, or heavy metal. Unlikely stars appeared. A former folk singer named John Denver captured the national pop charts with hits like "Country Roads," "Rocky Mountain High," "I'm Sorry," and "Back Home Again." He helped pave the way for the mellow sounds of Poco, Pure Prairie League, and New Riders of the Purple Sage. A little rockier than Denver, came the country-rock bands like the Eagles, a former backup group for Linda Ronstadt. Other groups traveled the folk-rock route, like Crosby, Stills, and Nash. Still other groups made the switch from hard rock to pop rock—Jefferson Airplane landed and then blasted off for the charts as the Jefferson Starship.

The seventies were a hurdy-gurdy mix of groups and styles. There was everything from Alice Cooper to Frank Zappa. The one thing they all had in common was quality in sound reproduction. Vast amounts were spent on production. Great strides were made in the processing of record albums. Players realized, after the deaths in the sixties, that staying on top meant having a clear mind. Audiences wouldn't go on paying cold cash to see rockers bumbling about in drug-induced hazes. To be number one you had to be sharp—and sober.

In spite of artists like Bruce Springsteen being heralded as the new king of rock, no one ever was. The eighties look to be much the same, though CBS Records' marketing of Springteen has given him phenomenal commercial success. Singer-songwriters like Jackson Browne and Billy Joel are now having great commercial success. These two seem to personify current mainstream rock. They are both thoughtful tunesmiths who write meaningful lyrics. But much more than mere entertainers, they are also communicators. Joel retains a street-wise attitude in spite of his stardom. In record and concert he sings that drugs "can make you die tonight." Browne, meanwhile, sings out of the seemingly soulless suburban morass that has trapped many of us. Though far from the only two rockers of the eighties (even the Monkees have made a comeback), they do capture the trend toward reflective songs on important issues. Paul Simon, Steve Winwood, Phil Collins, and Genesis are others. Of course, every time rock begins to take itself too seriously something comes along to put it in its place. In 1983 it was "Mickey" by Toni Basil. As a "Valley girl" would say, "Like totally *awesome!*"

The future of rock is far from certain. It changes daily. There are almost as many styles as there are listeners. Punk, new wave, pop, country, acid, and on and on. For a quick definition of each of these look at "Strata," at the back of the book. The large chunks of time and music dealt with in this chapter allow only generalized descriptions. Important names like Simon and Garfunkel, Bob Dylan, Carole King, Carly Simon, Aretha Franklin, Van Morrison, the B-52s have gone unmentioned. So have most of the historical events that happened at the same time. Though these are all interrelated, there is simply no way to do them justice in such a short space. The books listed in "Rockin' Resources" will help you learn the story of rock, if you need more than this chapter.

One thing all these omissions do is illustrate a point. They show us that rock is no tremendous Cyclops, possessing only one vision and obsessed with one goal. It doesn't all sound alike. Its stars once pumped gas, sang in church choirs, served in the armed forces, and did thousands of things that all of us do. It is as diverse as its audience.

If rock does have a goal, it is to make money. It is *commercial* entertainment. And make money it does. It has gone from a backwater art form, recorded on cheap vinyl in local warehouses, to the slickest mass-produced item in the world. It is a glowing testimony to American big business. It provides huge quantities of something for everybody. And what its listeners demand, they will be served.

The only thing certain about rock is that tomorrow's hit will sound different from yesterday's. Change is constant. Like any other music, rock has to change or stagnate. Who knows what the sounds of the future will be? But as Billy Joel sings, "It's still rock and roll to me."

1. To read the entire review, see either *Shaw's Music*, edited by Don H. Laurence and published by Dodd, Mead, or "A Shavian Sampler," *Newsweek* (November 30, 1981), p. 100.

2. Dave Marsh and Kevin Stein, *The Book of Rock Lists* (New York: Dell Publishing Company, Inc., 1981), p. 302.

3
Right, Wrong, and Rock

Looking at the roots of rock and roll, its development, and different forms, we see that it is just one of many musical types. All music has a long and varied history, from its earliest beginnings to the sophisticated sounds of a symphony. Music is one way humans express themselves. From classical to country, and everything in between, music is the art of emotions and communication. Rock is no exception. Though it has at times been perverted—as have other forms—it is perverted by the sinfulness of the human heart, not direct intervention by the forces of evil. Why should they waste their time, when we humans have already made it fairly gross? But just as most expressions of our deepest feelings contain great beauty, so too are there worth and dignity in rock.

Music is never stagnant—it is always changing. As people and cultures change, so do musical forms. Many of the themes—love, joy, death, despair—remain constant, with only the presentation changing. One society may use much more percussion than another; still another may use orchestration in a different way. As noted, love is one of the many themes—and is an example of how stylistic differences abound. Playing compositions by Beethoven, the

Beatles, and Buck Owens at the same time allows a terrible cacophony to occur. But played separately, each, in its own way, is beautiful. Different, yes. Yet the subject is the same—love.

Since all music is expression, it all has a message. The message is where rock gets its heaviest criticism. The critics of rock say that, because of rock's evil lyrics, good Christian folk have no business anywhere near it. They say that the songs are suggestive—or downright dirty—and that they carry a message contrary to the Christian faith. Rock and roll is full of sex, drugs, booze, antisocial behavior—it's trashy and dangerous. In many ways they are right; there is a lot of garbage in rock and roll.

Rock and roll, however, is not the only place in modern life where anti-Christian mores are advocated. Most of these are so accepted by the majority of Christians that we never question their influence on us. We pass them off as mere entertainment; but they are much more than that. They are every bit as much agents of moral change as is rock music. And perhaps more dangerous, for they're not even seen as such.

Let's begin with TV. Tune your Sony to any of the three major networks on a weekday afternoon and you will see lives that are pointedly different from the sort that would be promoted from the pulpit. Soaps portray adultery, heavy drinking, free love, ruthlessness, and more as being okay, fun, and the norm. *Newsweek* magazine, in a report on "General Hospital," says:

> To the extent that some viewers look to soaps to tell them what real life is like, today's younger generation may enter adulthood with some very odd notions about what to expect. A recent survey of soap addicts at the University of Kentucky discovered that most of them grossly overestimated the proportion of doctors and

lawyers in the real world, as well as the incidence of emotional illness and divorce. Heavy exposure to soaps may also warp adolescent sexual attitudes. According to a study conducted by a team at Michigan State, teen-age soap viewers are likely to conclude that married couples virtually never engage in sex, while singles do almost nothing else.

After watching 65 hours of serials, the researchers found that nearly 80 percent of the scenes in which intercourse was suggested occurred between unmarried lovers—and only 6 percent involved marital partners.

A less clinical examination of the genre, reveals other distortions of reality that, though harmless enough by themselves, add up to a bizarre portrait of ordinary life. With few exceptions, the inhabitants of Soapland are all upper-middle-class Wasps with homes straight out of House Beautiful. Almost all the characters are related by either marriage or blood. No one has a plain name like Jim or Jane. These people carry such monikers as Sky and Raven ("The Edge of Night"), Sebastian and Althea ("The Doctors"), Lance and Nikki ("The Young and the Restless") and Justin and Ashley ("Texas"). No one ever washes dishes, vacuums a rug, makes the beds—or watches television.[1]

The settings of these stories are exotic and glamorous, with beautiful people who lead exciting lives of wealth and sophistication. Rarely is life presented as it really is for the majority of viewers. But then who among us live lives as exciting as those on the soaps? Not very many if promiscuity, alcoholism, and shady doings are what make life worth living. Yet that is what we are being sold.

And we are buying it. Soaps are no longer thought of as vehicles to sell cleaning products to bored housewives. Today they are geared to college students and young professionals. Students are known to cut class for their favorite soap, and young execs videotape them to watch after work. Soaps have their own fan clubs, T-shirts, magazines, and Christian viewers.

Not everyone watches soap operas, you say? Quite true—so let's take a look at prime-time TV. The hours from 8:00 to 11:00 P.M. are filled with all sorts of shows that thrive on titillation and innuendo. The networks talk about "jiggle" shows—and we all know what's jiggling. If a show is not geared toward sexploitation, then violence is its theme. A sample of one evening's listings in *TV Guide* includes one news magazine, two situation comedies, four sixty-minute dramas, one miniseries, and a movie. One of the sitcoms is about sex/love, two of the hour-long series focus around violence, and the rest are a combination of the two.[2] All of this is in prime time—8:00 to 11:00. Multiply this by three hundred and sixty-five and it's shocking. Only on television is violent crime the focus of everybody's job—be they doctor, lawyer, or fall guy. In prime time, as in the afternoon, we are being sold the idea that only the lives on television—filled with sex or violence or both—are exciting. Ours, by comparison, are drab and dull. Surely such sexual exploitation goes against the dignity of personhood that Jesus Christ gives. Is not the senseless violence that is portrayed contrary to the peace He brings? And this is just on network television. We're not talking about what can be seen on HBO, Cinemax, Showtime, MTV, and so on.

For all the bad of television, not many of us are ready to throw it out. There is a great deal of good programming—though one seems hard pressed to find it. The ability to see news happening, history being made, is thrilling, sometimes scary, and mind-expanding. Entertainment specials with stars we couldn't see any other way are delightful. Those of us who are sports nuts have the chance to cheer for our favorite teams without paying twenty dollars a seat and dodging drunks. There are shows that are uplifting and in-spiring and in line with the life-style we think is best. Tele-vision brings a slice of the world at large into every city and hamlet—something that wasn't possible in the not-too-dis-tant past. So, though it is a mixed blessing, the TV sits in the corner still. It's there because we choose carefully what we watch and then filter what we see through the eyes of faith. (For a more in-depth look at television, see my book *Stay Tuned.*)

Much has been written about the state of cinema in our society. Our attitudes toward it have become increasingly ambiguous. Films that would have once shocked a whole town are now routinely accepted. A look at your local news-paper's theater listings probably reveals this most clearly. The Sunday film listing for Indianapolis as I am writing has one G-rated movie, eight PGs, eleven Rs, and the Xs aren't worth counting. These are all first-run feature films at major theaters. I'm not including drive-ins, which seem to special-ize in shows like *Wanda Werewolf and the Milwaukee Machete Massacre* or *Sexy Stewardessses and Promiscuous Pilots Fly to Fin-land,* with ads that leave little to the imagination.

Even though the ratings are to be a guide, they often don't mean much. The comedy *Airplane,* rated PG, has one scene with a topless lady and another that implies oral sex. *Raiders of the Lost Ark,* the 1981 box-office smash, had extreme amounts of violence, with the baddies being impaled, hit by airplane propellers, and having their faces melt off. And on any given Friday or Saturday evening at 7:00 P.M. our local movie house, as long as the film is rated PG, is packed with young-un's, and I do mean young, dropped off by parents for a couple of hours of cheap baby-sitting. I'll guess that it's the same where you live.

So, in spite of the rating system—or perhaps because of it (more people will go to see an R than a PG)—many young

43

people regularly see movies filled with illicit sex, violence, and language we consider unwholesome. They not only see them, they don't have to sneak in to see them. The R rating is a laugh, as many teens under the restricted age go to these films and are never challenged by theater management. Many of these teens go to your church. Ask how many members of your youth group have been to an R-rated film and you'll be surprised. A prominent, young Christian told me how she had seen the movie *Porky's* five times and, after telling me, got up and gave her testimony to a packed congregation. I'm glad she was saved, but wish she was saved from *Porky's* as well as other things.

The more a film flaunts Christian values, the more people flock to it—especially young people. Summer films are specifically geared toward teens, with names like *Summer Loves*, *Spring Break*, *Getting It On*, and more. They are all rated R; and they are all financially successful. If the film looks exciting—or sexy—people flock to it. The moral content is not a deterrent. If it looks good, or the stars are favorites, it's popcorn and Jujube time. Jesus said that if our eye offends us we should pluck it out. We have decided to risk our eye.

On the other hand, many movies, like television shows, have redeeming social value. There are always fine films around. The Christian cinema-goer might have to look hard to find them; but they *are* there. They are not all fifty years old, either. Some fine Christian films have been featured at neighborhood theaters; films like *The Cross and the Switchblade* and *The Hiding Place*. *Chariots of Fire*, a film with an explicit Christian message, was not only shown, but actually acclaimed by film-goers and critics alike. It even won four Academy Awards. A more recent worthwhile film is *The Mission*.

Many secular films teach values the Christian community holds dear. George Lucas's *Star Wars* series urges viewers to refrain from the dark, or evil, side of "The Force." Though far from explicit Christianity, and not even endorsing religion, it is the age-old morality of good versus evil. Richard Attenborough's *Gandhi*, a ponderous, three-and-a-half-hour epic, showed millions of viewers a life far removed from our Western consumer- and money-oriented morals. To be sure, *Gandhi* does not point toward Jesus as the answer. But thinking, caring Christians realize by watching this film how far the actions of our lives are from the teachings of Jesus. And *Places in the Heart* has an ending that makes sense only to Christians.

So we accept cinema, as we do TV, with its blend of good and bad. It's a part of our culture—a part we influence by our attendance at good films and our nonattendance at the others. We use our intellect and our faith to help us make the hard choices when it comes to the place of movies in our lives.

Along with some television and cinema, modern advertising also leads an assault on Christian beliefs. The thrust of much of it is sex appeal. The use of sex to sell is obvious to all. In *I Can Sell You Anything*, Carl P. Wrighter's book about the influence of advertising, the adman devotes two paragraphs to the topic of sex and ads. His reason? "I don't see the necessity of belaboring the sex angle anymore. You've seen enough of it, everywhere. Pretty girls in bikinis have sold everything from cars to milk, and will doubtless continue to do so."[3]

Sex appeal is important to us Americans. If we don't have it, that means we are not with it. We all want to be "with it," don't we? We are encouraged to be slim, sexy, and attractive to others, for such attractiveness determines our worth. And we can only be slim, sexy, and attractive to others if we purchase what's being advertised. Want to look like Brooke Shields? Buy Calvin Klein jeans. Guys, want to be another Jim Palmer? Slip into some Jockey underwear. Woe be unto us if we do not fit the Madison Avenue image, for then we are condemned for looking like we do—or not having the money to buy the looks we need. Advertisers dictate the length, color, and cut of our hair, the fit and name of our jeans, the correct body measurements, and countless other criteria that many of us cannot reach. Still we try, for we accept the image, we believe the lie. Why else are billions of backsides emblazoned with Gloria Vanderbilt, Oscar de la Renta, Zena—any name but the owner's own? You think that it is not true in Christian circles? Check out who is most popular in your high school Sunday school class or youth fellowship group. More often than not, it's those who are attractive and fashionable by society's standards. They are the ones the rest of us envy. "If I only looked like him" or "I wish I were built like her." We who call ourselves Christians should know better; but often we don't.

How can we condone the Madison Avenue hype? Especially when we realize that Jesus never cared what a person looked like on the outside. Jesus gave dignity, self-worth, and wholeness to those He came in contact with, regardless of how they were clothed. Surely none of us believes that Jesus set standards of how we were all to *look* before we were fit to be members of His Kingdom. Search the gospel long and hard, you will not find "the Christian dress code." Perhaps Jesus should have set one, but I guess He never realized how fully His people would buy into advertised attire. For not only have we condoned the Madison Avenue message, we have appropriated it. It is ours. Its styles are our styles. Its designs, our designs. Its ideal of young, slim, sexy, and attractive is our ideal. Before you say, "Well, maybe other Christians, but not me," listen to what Wrighter has to say.

    . . . every day, in hundreds of ways, we are
    selling you products on a logical, intellectual,
    factual basis. And you are being per-
    suaded. . . . you are being convinced—slowly,

carefully, logically convinced to make a
conscious decision to alter or change your
buying habits. You are being taught to buy false
eyelashes, order automatic transmissions, vote
for candidates, invest in mutual funds. There is
a great mythology in America that advertising
has, at best, a negligible influence on you.
Nothing could be further from the truth.
Today's advertising industry is the most potent
and powerful mass marketing and
merchandising instrument devised by man.

The truth of it is, advertising can sell you
anything.[4]

This sort of power is frightening; and our response is not
healthy, wise, or Christian. Our exclusion of those who do
not fit is a painful reality. We are all aware of people who
would be made to feel uncomfortable about the way they
looked or dressed if they were to turn up in one of the front
pews at our church some Sunday morning. This sort of exclusion—intended or not—is in direct opposition to the
gospel of Jesus. We know He never turned anyone away
because of outward appearance. Yet this happens frequently in the world of His followers—who have swallowed
Madison Avenue materialism.

Examples of the Christian community buying into this
worldly hype abound. The ads for Christian colleges in
magazines such as *Campus Life, Group,* and *Eternity* feature
pictures of students who could easily grace magazines like
Seventeen. They are attractive and fashionable, obviously
headed for success. You want to be like them? Come to our
college.

Likewise, the marketing of contemporary Christian music
reeks with fashion. Recording artists' photos show appeal-

ing, gorgeous singers. Stage apparel is carefully considered and up-to-date. Don't want to appear "out of it," you know.

Smiling at us from all sorts of Christian magazines, books, records, and posters are those whom the world would call glamorous. Not that there is anything wrong with beauty. After all, God created a beautiful world. But after a time it begins to seem as if only those who are young, handsome, dressed right, and have straight teeth get to sing on Christian records, appear in Christian college ads, or serve in important roles. What is to become of those of us who don't fit the image? The question may seem a bit extreme, but when was the last time you saw someone really physically ugly, but capable, do something for the Lord that got good public exposure? We have sanitized the secular system and made it our own.

Television, movies, and advertising are not the only corrupting influences that we accept as normal and necessary in our modern-day living. Music is also such an influence. But I am not talking about rock music. Turn on the radio and you will hear a multitude of musical styles. There is middle-of-the-road, beautiful music (also known as supermarket or dentist office music or Musak), rock, and country-western. More could be listed, but these are the major categories. Many of the styles are "crossing over"—that is, having no clear line between one style and another. Crossing over is when black star Janet Jackson's "When I Think of You" is on *Billboard's* Hot 100, Adult Contemporary, and Black Singles charts all at the same time. With crossing over, many former musical distinctions are becoming blurred. Rock still continues to be singled out as the carrier of the low morals plague. A closer look shows that the other forms are not 99 and 44/100 percent pure either.

Let's look at country-western first. Though hailed as the music of America, sprung fresh from the soil of the New World, C & W is no haven of holiness. Since early in its history, the mainstay themes have been cheating spouses, hard-drinking heroes, fistfights in crowded barrooms, and cruising in pickup trucks. While the pickup truck theme seems innocent enough, it is often the vehicle that drives the singer to the drunken fistfight with his cheating spouse. Seriously though, C & W has come a long way from the days of pure bluegrass and lonesome cowboys. The trip has been largely downhill. Some titles like "Heaven's Just a Sin Away," "Unwed Fathers," and "She Feels Like a New Man Tonight" give a clue to the direction taken. Yet many who condemn rock care little about the moral decline of C & W. After all, many C & W artists close their set with a gospel song or two. Surely that shows where their hearts are.

Middle-of-the-road, sometimes known as adult contemporary, is not much better. Nor is black or soul music, with songs like "Sexual Healing" by Marvin Gaye. Even classical music has had its moments in the past—such as when Stravinsky's "Rites of Spring" was played for the first time and the audience rioted in an emotional frenzy.

If we want to be fair, we cannot single rock out as the big moral meany, out to pervert society. The influences of television, cinema, advertising, and other musical forms are all around us. We have often tolerated the bad in these because they can also present much good. We do not, and should not, accept everything that is given to us. We have learned to be sensitive and selective. We screen the bad—and avoid it. We try to be sensitive to the needs that are shown and respond to them in the name of Jesus. We condemn the objectionable and rejoice in the good.

The same needs to be true of our attitude toward rock and roll. We need to be able to recognize that there is good as well as bad, encouraging listeners to be sensitive and aware. The time for a closed-minded castigating of a whole form of cultural expression is over. Part of that is because—largely due to the crossover phenomenon—the old musical barriers have come tumbling down. There will always be C & W, black, and rock-and-roll hits. But the good and evil distinctions become less clear as the lines of demarcation blur. That is not to say that we fling our arms open, joyfully embracing all that flows forth from the FM. Much of it is not worth embracing; but neither is it all worth trashing.

Admitting that rock and roll has its share of sex, drugs, violence, and cheap thrills—as do all the aforementioned villains—the next question has to be *Why?* What is the music trying to say, and why are certain subjects so prevalent in the rock format? What should my response be?

Rock is largely the music of a generation—youth. This premise will be discussed more fully in a later chapter. Suffice it to say that rock is the music of the young. As such, it expresses their concerns, needs, desires, and questions. Ralph Gleason, in *The American Scholar*, says, "For the reality of what's happening today in America, we must go to rock and roll, to popular music."

Since rock lyrics refer frequently to sex and drugs, is this the reality of young America? Is this what's on young people's minds? Yes—in the same way these concerns are on all of our minds. Rock is frank enough to bring it out into the open. That makes us older types uncomfortable. But all of us who care about life deal with these topics. We discuss them and try to discover how they fit into the larger arena of life. We don't think about them to the exclusion of everything else. Neither does rock and roll. Kids just have questions; questions that often make adults uneasy. They want to know about life and how it is to be lived and how it fits together. Since strong sexual feelings are going on inside them, it's natural that this is an item of discussion. We'd suspect something was wrong if it weren't.

Growing up was never easy, and it's harder today. The *adults* who control television, movies, advertising, *and rock music* push sex and thrills at teens. Adults may not watch or listen to it, but they *are* willing to produce and market it since it increases the profit margin and fattens the wallet. Just as many adults are seduced by soaps and jiggle shows, so too are many of the kids mesmerized by raunchy rock. Why should they be any different in this regard from their adult examples? Adults in marketing and sales know they aren't, so they produce music that appeals. And while it may be played by young performers, it's usually controlled by middle-aged money-makers—the agents, producers, and record company executives. It sells because it's aimed and typed to a rich, young, questioning, mobile, and somewhat confused generation.

As noted earlier, some themes seem to be more dominant in rock than in other musical forms. They are sex, drugs, and cheap thrills. Before condemning them for being there, lets take a look at *why* they are there in the first place.

The selling of sex in song—especially rock—is a good starting point. It would be foolish to deny that there is a lot of sex in rock. But sex in songs is nothing new. Even some real oldies have a suggestive nature. At your next friendly sing-along, listen to the lyrics of "My Wild Irish Rose," or how about Cole Porter's "Let's Do It." No one notices the innuendos anymore, we don't listen to the lyrics. Besides, they are harmless enough.

These are the same arguments young people use about rock. They don't really pay any attention to the lyrics, they just like the beat. To be sure, the sexual undertones of the music of the past are overtones in rock. What was only hinted at before, is now blatant. It's in the open and shouted out loud. Sometimes the lyrics are downright crude. Why the emphasis on sex? Is it because nothing is sacred anymore and going to bed with a lover is seen as no big deal? No. It's the opposite. The kids today are looking for something sacred—though many don't realize it consciously. They are looking for something that lasts, something they can put their trust in. Going to bed with someone is extremely important to them (at least to most of them). And it is more than just cheap curiosity about what's going on.

Sex is the most intimate relationship a man and a woman can share. It is special and unique. The feelings of closeness, safety, giving, and love are unparalleled. Christians extol the beauty of marital sexual activity. Teens hear this. That's why they buy and listen to records about love and sex. It's because in the love/sex relationships on vinyl they hear that their need for intimacy will be met. They hear that in sex there is love and passion. That is the joy—and the sorrow—of sex in rock and roll.

It is the joy because it's true. Love and sex are fulfilling. They are a tidal wave that washes over lovers and binds and renews them. A relationship between a man and a woman in which love and sex are melded is a beautiful thing—sustaining, recreating, making all things seem new and troubles far away. And that is how God wants it to be; that's how it was planned. Inside of marriage. Aha! The catch that is always thrown in! This catch is what most irritates teens. Their desires are so great; but they are not married, nor do most of them want to be yet. Why the big NO?

The love and sex that the Christian community and the Bible commend is based on love for God and the other person. Components of this love include sharing, trust, and, above all, commitment. This commitment, this decision to love forever, is the main ingredient for true joy in love and sex. Total giving of oneself to another is impossible unless both parties are committed. We all need to know that when we offer ourselves we will not be rejected—or used. This is especially true in sex. To be truly free and able to enjoy the sensuousness of sex means that you can trust the person to whom you are giving yourself. That trust develops only in a committed relationship. Without commitment to each other, there is no trust or responsibility. You may totally give yourself—only to find your name and phone number on bathroom walls or in smutty locker room conversations. This lack of commitment is the sorrow of sex in rock.

It is the sorrow because it implies intimacy and ecstasy—all free from commitment. "If it feels good, do it." The songs are about one-night stands or secretive sex. Commitment is unrequired. You'll have *your* needs met, and that's what's important. But, in fact, it's only an illusion. Some temporary physical craving may be satisfied, but the need for intimacy, for closeness, won't. It just can't happen in the back of a van, because you can never be quite sure that she won't find somebody with a neater car or more money, or that he won't stumble onto someone who's more beautiful. And you'll be alone again. The quest for intimacy will start all over. Partners prowl for other partners, looking for one who will live up to the legend of the songs on the radio. Somehow it's never quite as thrilling as the songs on the stereo say. Sex becomes disappointing and frustrating. The perfect partner—apart from a relationship of commitment—does not exist. Without commitment, people cease to be people, existing only as objects of gratification. Instead of sensual happiness and bliss, loneliness is the norm. Love dies—both for partners and *self.* There is no one you can be yourself with because you don't trust anybody enough to let them see the real you. All that is left is disillusionment with self and others—feelings of betrayal and a deepening hunger for love and intimacy.

Sex is wonderful. But the methods rock recommends bring you nowhere but down; they turn the joy of sex into the lie of lust. And loneliness is already the greatest affliction of adolescence—devastating more teens than does acne.

This loneliness is the reason that sex is such a popular topic in rock. There is much talk today about how society is full of lonely, alienated people. This is just as true for teens as it is for adults. Our homes, schools, and churches are filled with teens who feel unlovely, unloved, or both. They want to be loved. They crave closeness and security. Intimacy is the need, "please love me" is the cry. That's why there's so much sex in rock and roll—it offers easy intimacy. The method it advocates, however, usually leads to despair.

Although the influence of illegal drugs on rock is not as widespread as it once was, it is still present—especially if you consider alcohol a drug. As sex is to loneliness in the Top 40, so drugs are to desperation. Considering the state of our economy, the ever-present threat of nuclear annihilation, and all the world's other woes, what's not to be desperate about? Let's face it, reality can be pretty ugly. And depressing. Without an anchor or safe harbor on this stormy sea called living, many young people wonder if there's any use in going on. Some choose not to.

Newsweek reports that every year five thousand teens kill themselves, with another *half a million* trying to but not succeeding. That's a 300 percent increase since 1955.[5] The reasons are many—breakup of families, competitiveness in school and the job market, declining religious values—all the symptoms of a society that seems itself to be committing slow suicide. Many of these kids come from homes where they've always had everything they've needed—at least as far as material possessions go. In Plano, Texas, called "the quintessential Sun Belt City" by the *Los Angeles Times*, we find a booming, beautiful city, with more than its share of $250,000 homes and teenagers who drive their own Camaros and Corvettes to school. Yet, in the first eight months of 1983, this town of almost ninety thousand had four suicides and sixteen attempts. All this in one sparkling suburb.

Of course, most teens don't try to kill themselves, but the pressures are still there. They need ways to cope. Getting high or drunk is one way to do it. Drunk or high, your

54

problems pale in relation to how you feel "right now." When you're bombed, what's to bother you? And that is the adult approach. Mom and Pop have a martini (or two or three) to unwind at the end of the day. Why shouldn't the kids imitate what they've seen?

More people are leading lives of quiet desperation than we can imagine. After all, there are more of us than ever before. Thus we have more desperate young people. All of society's problems seem multiplied when you are young. Unemployment is higher for your age group. So are crime statistics, traffic deaths, and suicides. There is fierce competition everywhere for everything. There are so many young people—all after the same colleges, jobs, goods, services, and so on. Only the lucky, clever, and competitive shall inherit them. It's a time when many teens are looking for escape. When the song is about getting stoned, rock is telling you how to roll.

Along with sex and drugs, thrills have also been a major rock theme. The types advocated have been many—from hot rods to disco, from surfing to Rocky Mountain highs. Why thrills? Because modern life is so boring. Never in the history of humankind have so many people had so much—and not known what to do with it. This is especially true of leisure time. While our ancestors used almost every moment either eking out a living or sleeping for the next day's work, we have seemingly endless amounts of hours to do with as we want. With this increase in leisure time, you would think that people would finally be able to get out and *do* the things they want. Yet, the vast majority of us sit. We watch sports—not play them. We watch concerts on TV—not play the piano or sing ourselves. We gaze at gazelles on "Wild Kingdom" instead of at the local zoo. We watch families too—like the Huxtables on "The Cosby Show" or the Keatons on "Family Ties"—while our own fall apart. We have become a nation of bored sitters. We are bored with our jobs, our schools, our homes, ourselves. So we watch television. TV offers thrills and chills; and it does so in instant replays on four-foot-wide screens. If we get bored with network programming, we can entertain ourselves with video discs, videotapes, or video games. We live our lives in front of a Cyclops who demands our attention; and we give it willingly, except during commercial breaks when we go to get a snack. The excitement we can't find in our own lives can be found on "Miami Vice" or "Max Headroom." The lives on channel 4 are much more exciting than our own.

The same is true of rock. It's as thrilling and free as the TV. In the past we've been offered races in our little "409" out by "Dead Man's Curve" on the way to "Surf City." Today is no different. Through the thrills on the radio we can experience the things we dare not do ourselves. Want a thrill, a cure for the boredom that always seems to be lurking nearby? Go to the radio, friend, and live someone else's thrills. Live them in your dreams—maybe then your own life won't seem so dull.

That is why there are thrills in the radio. Because listeners are so bored with their own lives. The main themes exist to answer a need. Sex equals intimacy, drugs help one cope with desperate days, and thrills cancel our boredom. That sex, drugs, and thrills are presented in the way they are, troubles many Christians. And rightly so. Many of these ideas go against Christian standards. It is important for us to remember why they keep popping up. We need to keep in mind the loneliness, despair, and boredom.

A careful listener recognizes that rock is often a music of sadness or lament. In spite of a moving, pulsating beat, much of it is not happy. It speaks of broken lives and relationships. It questions everything. It demands to know why life is that way and often screams out in anguish. This may make us uncomfortable. But it is the cry of youth. It demands to be heard—and it will be.

We also need to realize that not all rock is about sex, drugs, and cheap thrills. There are some great rock songs. If you question that, just turn on your local "beautiful" music station. Many of the songs played there are former rock hits. The strings will be on violins and cellos instead of guitars, and there will be a whole percussion section instead of a drum set, but the songs are the same. They've been rerecorded and arranged this way because they are good. Classics like "Yesterday," "Killing Me Softly With His Song," and "Cherish" are former Top 40 rockers. There is much good music in rock.

We don't have to wait until tomorrow's arranger knocks off some of the rough edges and hires the London Symphony to find it all either. Much of it is great the way it is. The words are as moving as the melodies and have a great deal to say that is commendable and worthwhile. Dan Fogelberg's 1979 hit "Longer" is an example.

> . . . *Through the years as the fire*
> *Starts to mellow,*
> *Burning lines in the book of our lives,*
> *Though the binding cracks and the*
> *Pages start to yellow,*
> *I'll be in love with you.*
> *Longer than there've been fishes*
> *In the ocean,*
> *Higher than any bird ever flew,*
> *Longer than there've been stars*
> *Up in the heavens,*
> *I've been in love with you.*
> *I am in love with you.*

This song, as performed by Fogelberg, is a beautiful song about love *and* commitment. These are values we Christians cherish greatly. The song was a hit—good message and all.

It's been rerecorded by many others and is often sung at weddings. But even in its original pop rock form, it is a good song, well arranged, with most of the instruments featured being played by the singer/composer himself—Dan Fogelberg. We need to applaud and support such songs and their popularity.

There are many good rock songs—songs that sensitize our hearts and minds. They bring to our attention the crying need the world has for a Christian response.

The lists of good and bad could go on forever. Sex, true love, compassion, violence, drugs, and commitment are all among the subjects of the songs. That is because people are thinking about these issues. We need to unplug our ears and minds long enough to hear what's really being said. We may find ourselves with new insights. We'll see new ways to respond to the human condition. We Christians claim to have found joy and a purpose in living. We need to quit "exaggerating this, exaggerating that," as Paul Simon sang, and have some fun. And in the process, show some needy people what "fun" really is.

---

1. "Television's Hottest Show," *Newsweek* (September 29, 1981), p. 64.

2. *TV Guide*, Indianapolis area listings, September 26–October 2, 1981, pp. 113–118.

3. Carl P. Wrighter, *I Can Sell You Anything* (New York: Ballantine Books, 1972), p. 113.

4. Ibid., p. 2.

5. "Teen-age Suicide in the Sun Belt," *Newsweek* (August 15, 1983), p. 70.

4
Rockin' Rebels?

While their music and most of their lyrics
may be blandly unobjectionable, the life-styles
they flaunt make the purchase of an ABBA
album a possible subsidy of public promiscuity.[1]

In the above quote, Bob Larson echoes the concern of many Christians. Why support life-styles contrary to Christian faith? Besides the use of drugs and sex as major themes in the songs, they seem also to be a major part of rock musicians' life-styles. *People* and *Us* magazines always seem to have some feature on the shocking behavior of this or that rock star. Their lives, we are told by people like Larson, are crammed full of illicit sex, drugs, booze, and other shady dealings. Since they have worldwide attention, the influence they wield is mighty. Their immorality will lead others astray. We don't want to make them rich enough to continue these despicable life-styles. So don't buy rock records.

No doubt the lives of some rock and rollers are awful. The use of alcohol and drugs has been a topic of discussion since rock's early days. Rock's past is littered with numbing evidence of drug abuse in rock circles. But before we condemn out of hand, let's look at a few things.

The world of rock music is like the inside of a pressure cooker under which the heat is gradually being increased. While it appears to the outsider to be a life full of the joys of recording and performing, it is also a world of cutthroat competition. Most bands are not overnight successes, nor will they ever be superstars. They work away at their trade, playing small clubs, colleges, and weddings. Some get lucky, if lucky is the word. They land a recording contract with a major label. But the sad fact is that they are still at the bottom of the heap; no one has ever heard of them. They are just one of hundreds of new groups "discovered" every year. And if a listening audience doesn't discover them, they'll be placed in the sale rack at the local record store, wholesaled out at $2.99.

Let's say the improbable happens. They gain an audience. Their single goes gold. Their video is on heavy rotation on MTV. All of a sudden they are the hottest item in America. Transformed from a band with time on their hands, now they've got no time at all. The record company wants to rush them back into the studio for a follow-up hit video. Concert promoters see halls they can fill with screaming fans for fifteen, twenty, or even thirty dollars a seat. Appearances on "American Bandstand" and "Saturday Night Live" are booked. They are on the road. Endless bus rides and airplane trips to endless cities with endless auditoriums. Play at night, grab a bus seat, try to sleep, ride all day, set up and rehearse in the evening, play at night, grab a bus seat, . . . Jackson Browne's *Running on Empty* album has captured for the listener the frustration and waste of life on the rock road.

For many young groups catapulted into the neon nightmare of live rock, the strain is incredible. Days, as well as towns and fans, become a blur. A permanent weariness seems to settle on the soul. It's harder and harder to "get up," feel alive, for the night's performance. So someone offers them something to get them up—and it works. The chemical rush makes them feel vital and alive. After the show, back on the bus, they are still up, they can't seem to come down. But that's okay—there are pills to bring you down, too. Pills cure all ills. Up or down, just spin around, up or down. The circle is complete. For many that's too late. Unable to cope, they turn to harder and harder drugs. Then they die.

It's not only the good who die young, or only the young who die, however. Though Jimi Hendrix, Janis Joplin, Tommy Bolin, and Keith Moon were young, the most famous victim of drugs was not. Far from an overeager young performer unable to cope with the pressures of success, Elvis was old (by rock standards), overweight, and unable to cope with his fading glory. He went to his friendly doctor for help. Dr. George Nickopoulos gave Elvis something to make him feel better. It took the Tennessee Medical Board eight legal-size pages to list all the drugs Nickopoulos prescribed for Presley—and all within the last eighteen months of his life. Included on the list are Valium and Hydrochloride cocaine. The list is staggering. It was also tragic in its consequences.

Certainly less dramatic, but as certainly more important, than these stories of rockers using drugs, are the stories of those who aren't. Some, like Little Richard and Pete Townshend of the Who, once were. Now they are reformed drug users, who discourage drug reliance on the part of their peers. Bruce Springsteen, Ted Nugent, and Frank Zappa, while varying a great deal in musical format, openly disdain drug use—by rock stars or anybody. Songs like "Sam Stone" by John Prine or Neil Young's "The Needle and the Damage Done" graphically illustrate the futility and desperation of drugs as a way out. Many rockers have seen their friends' lives broken and destroyed by drugs and therefore urge kids to leave the stuff alone. That is, unless they want to end up as a snow-blind friend.

As noted in chapter 2, many performers avoid drugs because of the deaths of Morrison, Hendrix, and Joplin at the heights of their careers. Drugs impair the ability to perform. Drugs can kill. Performing, living, and being at the top is every rock star's dream. That's what all the long hours practicing in an old garage or musty basement were for. That's why they're willing to play in local coffeehouses and clubs. Because they dream of being number one someday. Rick Cua, former bassist for the Outlaws, says, "I wanted to get to the top, to be the best (who doesn't?). . . ."[2] That's the goal. The road taken is hard and bumpy. Today's rock and rollers, for the most part, are too smart to throw it all away for some temporary highs. You can't stay on top and be stoned.

While drug abuse was once a large part of the rock scene, it could hardly be more prevalent there than in the rest of our society. That statement may be a bit bold, but I believe it is true. A government-sponsored study by the Research Triangle Institute showed that drug use in all lines of work cost the American economy $25.8 billion in 1983. Of that amount, $16.6 billion was in lost productivity.[3] From assembly lines to corporate boardrooms to nuclear power plants to hospitals, no part of the modern American work force is free from drug abuse. The Digital Equipment Corporation (the computer people) has full-time drug and alcohol abuse counselors at twenty-five plant locations. Other companies are following suit. Still others are using guard dogs trained to sniff out drugs. Even the "pure" National Football League has been rocked by drug scandal. Always presenting a positive, clean-cut image for its young fans, the NFL was exposed to have players who used illegal drugs. Some players were suspended, and implications abounded that more should have been. Unfortunate as it is, drug use and abuse is a part of our society. Why else is urinalysis in sports and business even considered? That is not to say that it involves most people. The majority of us have more sense or stamina. It certainly isn't okay. It's a problem. One that all society, not just rock society, needs to face up to.

In addition to drugs, the sexual behavior of rock stars is also a concern. The exploits of groups and groupies have always made good copy for fan magazines and tabloids. Such blatant disregard for sensible sexual mores has shocked many of us. Sexual activity seems to come in hetero, homo, or combinations of the two. David Bowie and Elton John both made statements early in their careers to the effect that they were bisexual. Bowie has since said that he was young, made the remarks without thinking, and regrets he made them. But they still stick in the public's mind.

We all know that rock stars don't have a corner on the immoral sexual behavior market. Why then is such a big deal made of it? Christians don't like it because it goes against our standards. So we, rightfully, make a big deal of it. The stars and their agents don't find our noise about it troublesome at all. They don't want their exploits kept private.

There are a number of reasons why. The first is that the public won't let them. There is no such thing as a private star. People want to know what they eat and drink, how they dress, where they live, and who they sleep with. Magazines like *People* cater to the fans' need to know *everything* about their favorite star. So even if there is the same proportion of sexual strangeness in the rest of the world, it seems to be concentrated in the rock world, because they get the press. Stars don't have the same privacy for their immorality we common folk do.

Second, the public welcomes whatever a celebrity says with an attitude approaching awe. Stars are treated as if they were privy to some great truths that we mere mortals only strive for. The world clamors for someone to say how things are and how they should be. Where once we turned to those we respected—teachers, parents, preachers—for advice, we now turn to media stars. It's as if, just by being on TV, radio, or records, they have instantly acquired vast amounts of knowledge. They have become more than they were.

While this is especially true in the secular world, it is true in the Christian world as well. What radio and TV preachers say is often deemed loftier and more important than the local pastor's sermon. While pastoring one congregation, I had some people who often told me that, although what I had said was mostly correct, according to the sermon of Brother So and So on the radio, I was wrong on a number of things. It didn't matter that I had the education and he did not. It mattered not that I spoke of orthodox, evangelical doctrine and he his own brand of belief. What mattered was that he was Brother So and So on the radio, and I was only the pastor in the pulpit. The fans of Christian celebrities are as much in evidence as fans who hang on to Jon Bon Jovi's every word.

Finally, and probably most important, is shock value. Americans love to be shocked. We don't like admitting it, but it's true. What else accounts for the huge success of movies like *Hallowe'en* and *Friday, the 13th*? And the never-ending sequels like *Hallowe'en XXII* and *Friday the 13th—Jason Still Lives and Comes Back With His Grandson!!!* Groups like Iron Maiden with their outrageous acts also shock—and shock sells. If marketing reps fail to gain our attention with flash pots and onstage antics, how about some juicy offstage revelation?

Much of what rock stars say should be seen for what it is—pure hype. Everyone knows Americans have an intense preoccupation with sex. We may giggle and deny it, but the evidence is all around us. All we need do is look at the contents of our advertising, television, and radio programming.

Rock stars and their promoters want us to buy their product. So they—like everyone else—use sex to sell it. It may be bizarre sex, but it sells records.

These looks at sex and drugs in the lives of rock stars are not meant to excuse. Far from it. Rock and rollers, like all of us, are accountable to God for their actions. But it is important to look at these moral issues in their lives to help us understand them as people, and to help us be consistent in our relations with the world.

Bob Larson, in the piece that opens this chapter, implies that buying rock records by people who are living immorally means we'll support their life-styles. Therefore, we shouldn't buy rock records. But how far are we willing to take this stand? Abuse of drugs and sex are evident in all segments of our society. Do we quit buying Fords because some assemblers in Dearborn are on drugs? Will we stop watching the New York Mets because Dwight Gooden had a cocaine addiction? Is it time to sell our stocks and bonds because stockbrokers are snorting coke? Perhaps we should ignore all congressional action. After all, two representatives were having sex with their pages. And one of those affairs was homosexual.

These suggestions are a bit extreme. No one would seriously consider them. After all, an assembler on drugs is just one man among many. But Larson's concept of supporting immorality by purchasing a rock record is no less true when applied to buying an auto that was partially assembled by an addict. The actions and attitudes of a minority should not negate the worth of the rest. If we are hesitant about boycotting cars, why is it so easy to condemn those who buy rock records?

Though the rock life-style is often looked at as "life in the fast lane," full of sex, drugs, and anything else imaginable, it is often not so. Take Rick Cua, mentioned earlier, as an example. Rock music is his craft, his livelihood, just as someone else's is accounting, assembling automobiles, or piloting planes. His children go to school like everyone else's. He has a wife (she helped him get the children). He occasionally cooks spaghetti dinners for the family. On Sunday, they go to church together. His is far from a life in the fast lane. His life sounds almost like ours—even boring.

Cua says, ". . . contrary to what a lot of people think about rock, there are plenty of us rock and roll singers and musicians who believe in God and practice our faith. Who says you can't play rock and roll and stand up for the Lord?"[4]

While rock has its perverts and addicts, it has its good guys as well. When the media accentuate the sinners, remember the saints. People like Donna Summer who have rediscovered their faith and Rick Cua who never lost his. Pray for these brothers and sisters in the faith, that they may help their lost and confused contemporaries. And give thanks that not all rockers are on a highway to hell.

---

1. Bob Larson, *Rock: Practical Help for Those Who Listen to the Words and Don't Like What They Hear* (Wheaton: Tyndale House Publishers, 1980), p. 123.

2. Rick Cua, "In God's Hands," *Guideposts* (September 1983), p. 20.

3. "Taking Drugs on the Job," *Newsweek* (August 22, 1983), p. 55.

4. Cua, "In God's Hands," p. 21.

5
Why Rock at All?

Though there is good rock, much of it is bad. Why listen? What is to be gained by putting up with something that we must be very cautious about? The good does not cancel out the bad—does it? Why subject ourselves to unwholesome ideas? These are hard questions that need to be asked. The answers will not be easy.

One answer is to turn it off. Simply shut the stereo down and throw the records and tapes away. If you like music, develop new musical interests and leave rock alone. That *is* a real option—though not a very popular one. You have to ask yourself why you are turning it off, though, if you want to make a good and lasting decision. Simply getting fed up and pitching the stuff in a moment of disgust will probably find you listening to it again in a few days.

Think about your decision to give up rock. Is it conviction or taste? There is a big difference between the two. Remember, taste is purely personal, conviction means taking a stand. If you feel that Christians have nothing to gain and everything to lose by listening to rock, you *should* shut it off. Deciding to turn it off because of spiritual conviction is an admirable decision.

Not listening has many benefits. First, you won't have to

be constantly on guard against ungodly and immoral messages in the airwaves. That in itself makes such a decision worthwhile. Second, you will find you have more time to do other things. Suddenly all the time you had spent listening to rock will be given to you like a present on your birthday. You will have more time to spend with your friends and family. Serving as a volunteer in a hospital or nursing home will be possible because of your increased free time. Use the time to get closer to God through Bible study and prayer.

A third benefit of not listening is more money. Since you won't be plunking down $8.98 or more for the album of the week, you will have more cold cash. Consider using the money for a ministry project, such as supporting a child through World Vision or some other good organization. Recordland won't really miss the money, but think of the difference you could make in a child's life.

Turning off rock won't win you any popularity contests. Your friends may think you have finally flipped out. But then, Jesus never said that following Him would be easy. If you are convinced that you shouldn't listen, don't. Your witness in this will help others who are struggling. If you decide to shut it off completely, don't apologize. Thank God for the wisdom He granted you and ask Him for the power to sustain you when times get rough. He will, you know.

If you like the style but are bothered by the lyrics, that too shows wisdom on your part. There is a lot of raunch in rock and roll. If you want the beat without the bad news, there is good news. You have a super option—contemporary Christian music (CCM). CCM, like regular rock, comes in a wide variety of musical flavors. You can choose from pop rock, new wave, jazz-oriented, folk rock, and more. The lyrics are usually based on Scripture and the sound quality is on a plane with most secular rock. CCM also provides a way to witness to your non-Christian friends by playing your favorite CCM records for them and getting their reactions to them. For more on CCM check out chapters 8 and 9.

Though there are reasons to shut rock off, there are also reasons not to. One is that rock is the music of a generation. Rock has always belonged to the young. It speaks to teens. It talks about the things they care about—love, sex, peace, war, and more. It deals with the needs of the world. We may not like the way it handles certain topics or the things it says, but it does force us to think about what it's saying. While it may be more comfortable to pretend we are ostriches and ignore the messages, we who follow Jesus need to learn to tackle tough issues head-on. Rock raises these issues.

Another reason that rock appeals is that it is not Mom and Dad's music. Mom and Dad don't like it, understand it, or listen to it. But then, kids don't like, understand, or listen to Lawrence Welk. For many teens, this second reason for listening is good enough. We all want something that sets our group apart, makes us different from any previous generation. Rock, with its infinite variety of styles, is a part of this. Levi's, Big Macs and fries, and scary movies are all identifiers—they all appeal more to the young than to the old. Within the young there are subgroups—the jocks, the brains, the band, the surfers (though they are few in Indiana), the dopers, and so on—who all have their badges of identity. Usually the one and only common denominator is rock. However, even rock is broken into many forms, depending on the groups. The band kids may like Toto more than the jocks who, in turn, like Bruce Springsteen more than the brains do. Rock music and teen years go hand in hand—and have since 1955.

This search for separate identity is not a sign of lack of love or respect for Mom and Dad. Teens still have deep feelings for the old folks; they just don't want to go to the same movies, parties, eateries, or whatever that their parents go to. It really is just a matter of establishing their own identities. This separateness is a rite of passage—a move into the adult world where we are called largely to be self-sufficient and independent. And it is not something new. Parents, try to remember the things you did as a teen; things which seemed perfectly natural to you, but your parents did not understand. Think back to tight-legged pants, poodle skirts, duck-tail haircuts, Fabian, and Dion and the Belmonts. Many of us think it would be great if kids would look as if they just stepped out of a "Leave It to Beaver" rerun. Even creepy Eddie Haskell was dressed nicely and didn't need a haircut. But we need to remember that there are some kids who do look and dress that way—and stand on street corners selling flowers for cults.

People do change as they get older. My father had recurring nightmares that I would still be wearing blue jeans, football jerseys, tennis shoes, and long hair when I reached his age. As I write this, I am wearing corduroys (with a crease even—how 'bout that, Mom!), a button-down shirt, loafers with a shine, and my hair is short on the sides and nearly gone on the top. My dad is the one with the Levi's and football jerseys; and I wish I had half the hair he does. Talk about changing times. But I still listen to, and like, rock and roll. He still likes the Boston Pops. We have both grown—and matured. In light of this I offer parents the following:

> **For temporary relief of inflammation due to minors:**
> **Repeat, "This, too, shall pass."**
> **Take as often as needed.**

Musical tastes, just like styles of dress and haircuts, change. Rock listened to often mellows with the person.

The format that was popular to a teen is often a pain in the ear when the person reaches old age (late twenties and early thirties). Devotees of Steppenwolf and other sixties and seventies "heavy metal" bands now make up the audience called adult contemporary, which tends to be much more mellow and laid back. The two styles are as different as the Beatles' own "I Want to Hold Your Hand" and "I Want You (She's So Heavy)," which themselves show a progression in musical form. The groups, with a few notable exceptions like the Rolling Stones, have also matured and mellowed with age. The Jefferson Airplane is now a Starship with a much smoother sound. Groups even display increasing social consciousness. While the Jefferson Airplane may have advocated drug use in the late sixties, they recently raised $10,000 for the Walden House drug rehabilitation center in San Francisco.

Since rock was the music of people's youth, it will remain part of their lives. The change may be from punk to pop, but until senility sets in at thirty-three and a third, and they start asking, "Why do kids listen to that junk?" rock will be their music (after thirty-three there is an increasing urge to play only "golden oldies").

As mentioned earlier, rock often deals with the things kids are thinking about. The fifties theme could be expressed by Clyde McPhatter's "Without Love (There Is Nothing)," that and being "At the Hop" and doing "The Twist" and "The Stroll." The early sixties found the Beach Boys and their clones cruising in "Little Deuce Coupes" looking for "Endless Summers" filled with "California Girls." The Vietnam War, racial tension, and campus unrest spawned songs like "Universal Soldier," "Abraham, Martin, and John," and "A Hard Rain's A-Gonna Fall." As television screens brought the pain, blood, and body counts of modern war into our living rooms, so too did radio bring songs of anger and protest. These were songs by an angry generation, fed up with being made into machines of destruction. The protest songs were harsh and grating, like the subjects they spoke out against. They screamed and got your attention.

If the sixties screamed, the seventies soared. As society changed, so did rock. Many songs called for simple life and Rocky Mountain highs. This back-to-nature music by John Denver and others floats like the eagles and wind it celebrates. While it was not rock like Presley or the Beatles, it captured the Hot 100 and the hearts of listeners. Ex-Beatle John Lennon asked us to "Imagine" a world of peace and harmony. The late seventies saw romantic love reemerge as a major theme, with songs like "You Light Up My Life." Now in the eighties, concerns about the homeless and nostalgia for the sixties are evident in songs like "Hands Across America" and the reemergence of the Monkees. We can be sure that the music of the future will reflect the future's fears. If there is war or rumor of war, look for protest songs. If there seems to be more turmoil than usual, we will hear songs about safety and security. If you want to know what is on rockers' minds, listen to the music. The message will come through clearly.

Besides speaking to needs and concerns, rock is just plain fun. You can't deny it. It's infectious. Rock grabs you by the ears, slips into your spine, travels to your feet, and makes you tap your toes. It moves your mouth and flicks your fingers. It invites response. You can't sit still. Nothing is harder on a group of kids than turning on a Top 40 hit and telling them they can't sing along. It is inhumane. It's cruel. They will sit there fuming and fidgeting, then start lip-synching when they think nobody's looking, a few words will weasel their way out, till finally the whole group is singing. These jock-types whose faces go red and voices go away in the Youth Choir, will be bellowing the words as loud as they can. No reason for timidity here. Those few (and they are few indeed) who recognize their inability to sing and choose not to inflict their voices on others' ears, will at least be bopping around in their seats. It is nigh unto impossible to remain passive while listening to rock.

Opponents to rock point to this as proof of its unwholesomeness. In chapter 4, I quoted Bob Larson, author of *Rock and Roll: The Devil's Diversion* and *The Day the Music Died*, who says that "there is a power and force in rock. It has the ability to immerse and totally envelop the listener."[1] He goes on to say that this is especially true in a live concert. Larson sees this as a major proof of rock's evilness.

"Ability to immerse and ... envelop. ..." What music doesn't? If emotional involvement makes a song bad, where would that leave school fight songs? Or alma maters? Country and western? Movie sound tracks? Hymns of the church? I admit that rock and roll involves me. So does Beethoven. So does the majesty and power of "A Mighty Fortress Is Our God." Granted, the intent of "Joyful, Joyful, We Adore Thee" and "Don't Go Breaking My Heart" are going in two different directions, but *both* have the power to move and excite. Involvement is necessary for all music.

We all have been places where the music captured us and took us along. Sitting in darkened cinemas, tennis shoes glued to the floor by a mixture of candy and spilt soda, we sit transfixed by the music, knowing that something terrible is going to happen. We cringe, scream, or run out of the theater—shoes still stuck by our seats—at the time the music tells us to. Packed into bleachers at altitudes guaranteed to give nosebleeds, we watch tiny figures play baseball and jump to our feet screaming "Charge!" when the bugle sounds (something that scares the socks off peace-loving Quaker-types like me—especially when I'm yelling the loudest).

The other end of the musical spectrum finds us sitting in church. We wander in, take our seats, our minds full of last night's date, today's pot roast, this afternoon's NFL game. The organ begins sounding songs of praise. Soon hearts and minds are caught and rechanneled. A previously disparate group has been melded into a worshiping congregation.

All music has power. It can cheer us—or scare us. It can lead us into God's presence. Music can be our friend during lonely times, soothing our souls. Rock music is no exception. Its power to move does not make it evil.

Rock, in spite of frequently depressing lyrics, is fun. The back beat and melody line are contagious. Rock helps you to feel things that might otherwise be missed in the humdrum of everyday life. It is a refreshing alternative to boring lives played out to Muzak. The lively melodies of Huey Lewis and the News and similar groups bring a certain zest to the stereo. That is what rock is meant to be—just plain fun.

Too many find too much in too little—either pro *or* con. Rock does not harbor the answers to the deep questions of life. Neither is it one of the devil's weapons. Mick Jagger says: "The position of rock and roll in our subculture has become far too important, especially in the delving for philosophical content."[2]

Rock is entertainment. That is what it is meant to be. That and a money-maker for the artists and record companies. As long as it is seen as entertainment, it is in its right place. As entertainment it is usually successful—why else would people spend over $4 billion a year on records and tapes. You can be sure a record that is not entertaining will probably not make it onto *Billboard*'s Hot 100. It will quickly sink into oblivion.

As a place to find the answers to life's questions, it will be a disappointment. It does make us aware of some of the issues. But its answers are shallow—what else can they be with only three to five minutes of airplay?

We don't want to live without it. We don't have to. It is

fun and a part of the culture. That does not mean that it is all acceptable, but neither does it mean it is all trash. If we take the time to recognize the good and the bad, paying attention to what is going on lyrically, we don't have to live without it. But we do have to learn how to control it, not let it control us. That is the hard answer to the hard questions. The secret to listening well is looked at in the next chapter. The key is to remember our allegiance to Jesus. He is the one we don't want to live without.

_____

1. "Door Interview: Bob Larson," *The Wittenburg Door* (April-May 1979), p. 10.

2. Dave Marsh and Kevin Stein, *The Book of Rock Lists* (New York: Dell Publishing Company, Inc., 1981), p. 7.

6
Rock and Roll Without Losing Your Soul

Another title for this chapter could be "How Should We Listen?" For some the answer is simple—we shouldn't. Others of us, as we talked about in the last chapter, don't want to live without it. So we listen. Then someone tells us that rock is raunchy, or satanic, and good Christians do not listen to it. Then we feel guilty. And guilt is not one of the most pleasant feelings. I want to suggest a number of ways to listen to rock and avoid feeling guilty. Some are better than others, and one can even make us better disciples of Jesus. This section calls for you to respond and make decisions. Decisions are not always easy, and many times we would just as soon someone else made them for us. But if we let others decide how we will live, we may not be too happy with what they decide. Living for Jesus means making the choices He wants us to make, assured that He wants what is best for us. The choices may be tough ones. They are, however, choices that ensure we have a life worth living.

We can decide to quit listening. If we do so because of taste—we prefer Phil Collins over Conway Twitty—that's not hard to do. I made that decision long ago and now whenever Conway Twitty comes on, I shut the radio off and let the Twitty birds fly away. But if we really like Conway Twitty and can't stand Phil Collins, but object to Conway's song lyrics, that is a whole other thing. To love classical (or country or easy listening or jazz) and abhor rock makes for an easy decision—don't listen to rock. For others who really like rock as a musical style, the decision not to listen is harder than it was for you. What I am saying is, if you decide to shut off rock, don't look down on those who have not made the same decision you have. Examine your reasons for shutting it off. If it is because you prefer other styles, you have to allow others their styles.

If you are shutting it off because of content, you have some other questions you must deal with. What about television? Will you also be discriminating in what you watch? How about movies? After all television and cinema are both saturated with sexual immorality and violence. All about us there is evidence that society's way stands opposed to Christ's way.

I am not trying to make it difficult to give up listening to rock. I think that is an admirable position. I hope, if that is what you decide, that you will have the strength to take such a bold stand. What I am pressing you to be is a consistent witness. If you decry rock's immorality to your friends and then go see *Porky's II* with them, what sort of faith are you showing? I hate to say it, but that is hypocritical. We have to watch our witness, and make sure that all areas of our lives are in line with what we say. We want to glorify God—not embarrass Him.

The flip side to shutting rock off is listening to anything that comes out of the stereo. If it's Top 40 it must be good. Lots of people listen that way. Turn it on and let it play all day. The car radio's always blasting away as we bomb down the boulevard. Or we're sprawled out over the kitchen table with Algebra II, while a three-quarter-time hit beats away from the radio perched on top the fridge. Then we say, "Hey, I'm not really listening. The radio's just on, y'know, for background." It may be background, and we may think we are not listening, but we are. We are also learning.

Those words that float by our ears are influencing us. They really are. Repetition, after all, is the easiest way to learn. Baby learns "Patty Cake" because Momma says it over and over again, until it becomes part of Baby's thinking. Chances are you weren't taught "Jesus Loves Me" by sight-reading sheet music given you by a choir director. No, you learned it, because every Sunday in your kindergarten church school class your voice blended (sort of) with the other tiny voices, singing the words taught by elderly Mrs. Clark. This repetition is why we remember songs like "Jesus Loves Me" and Bible verses like John 3:16. We learn lots of things, including rock lyrics, by repetition. We may not like it—or even be aware of it. But we learn it.

The Top 40 at most radio stations is a Top 10 or Top 15. That is, while they may list a Top 40, based on sales and airplay, the station plays ten or fifteen of the forty much more regularly than the other twenty-five or thirty. These songs are put in a certain pattern—usually called heavy rotation—so that they are heard over and over again. To check this on your local radio station, find out what the number one song is (look at *Billboard* magazine or ask your station) and ask the station how many times that song will be played in a twenty-four-hour period. Then check number thirty-six; see how often it will be played. You'll find that you have a chance to hear number one much more than thirty-six. You'll hear it enough that you'll know the lyrics, whether you think you have listened or not. You may not be able to recite them in "Rock as Modern Poetry" class when Mr. Schmidlap calls on you, but when your backside hits the backseat of the Buick with the back beat blowing out the speakers, you will have total recall. You will *know* the words.

"You are what you eat" is a popular slogan from recent history. It implied that if you ate junk food you would turn into junk and if you ate health food you would be healthy. This is fairly true, though not literally. I mean, when is the last time you saw a six-foot-tall Twinkie stuffing quarters into Pole Position or a granola bar out jogging? (If you have then I recommend you quit reading this book and hop down to your optometrist and take a look at his eye chart.) There is a correlation between diet and behavior. When I subsist on hot dogs, chips, and sodas, I wear out quickly. The sugar and caffeine in soda may make me feel like my body could go on forever, but I can't. When I sit down to three square meals every day, I feel better—and look better. I'm not filling my body with empty (no nutritional value) calories, so I won't be wearing them somewhere around my middle. So, if I have convinced you that you are what you eat, let me take you one step further—you are what you hear.

You are what you hear. Like it or not, it is true. Are you pretty or ugly? Why do you answer the way you do? It's because you believe what people have told you. Our feelings about ourselves are based on what we have been told. Our self-image is reinforced, or destroyed, by what we hear most. People who constantly hear that they don't do it (whatever *it* might be) right, never will do it right. At least that is how it will seem to them. They will never measure up. Likewise, people who receive praise will do praiseworthy things and feel good about themselves. We are all like the trains in *The Little Engine That Could.* If we think we can, we can. If we think we can't, we can't. Either of these feelings comes largely through what we are told by our family, friends, and others.

When someone close to me first entered college, he took the required English course. This friend had always enjoyed

English (especially literature), was a good reader, a fairly bright student (though his grades didn't show it), and harbored a secret desire to be a writer. Freshman English destroyed all that. The professor told him that his writing was terrible, his thoughts boring, and to look into some other occupation. My friend was crushed. Eventually he dropped out of college with miserable grades.

My friend did go back to school, much later and at another college. Since writing was out, he took art and became a fair painter. But his desire was still to write. It found its expression in term papers and independent studies. Professors told him how well he wrote—even an English professor. He then wrote some short book reviews for publication. They were accepted. So were his interviews, and later even books. He still gets rejection slips, but because of supportive people finally overriding a negative one—the first professor—he still writes. The writer friend? It's me.

It is up to you to decide whether or not you like the way I write. I hope you do. If you don't, well, I wish you did. Either way, I intend to keep writing. I can because of the positive, repeated reinforcement I get. I write because people believed in me and told me I could. And I can.

What have repetition and reinforcement got to do with rock and roll? Everything. We repeatedly hear, via the airwaves, that what the Church says is wrong, is really all right. Whose standards do you accept? God's or rock's? Where do your moral stands come from? Mom and Dad? friends? church? rock? the Bible? Be honest—especially with yourself. Don't give the answer you think I want to hear or your youth pastor would approve of. Do you echo the Christian answer and yet question it deep down inside?

What goes into us has tremendous influence on the thoughts and actions that come out. Look at your views on premarital sex. Is it okay to sleep with your boyfriend or girl friend even if you are not married, as long as you love each other? Is it? That's what rock says. And so do a lot of Christian kids—kids like you. Reverend Steve Clapp in *Teenage Sexuality: A Crisis and an Opportunity for the Church* writes:

> Though there were some exceptions, in general, I found that what was true for a secular population of teenagers in California was true for a church active population of teenagers in the midwest. [Aaron] Hass found that 56% of the males and 44% of the females in his study had experienced sexual intercourse by the age of eighteen. In my sample, 59% of the [church active] males and 42% of the [church active] females had experienced sexual intercourse by eighteen.[1]

The real question for us is not the similarities, but where did the attitudes come from?

If the songs on the radio, day in and day out, say sex outside of marriage is okay, and, one day a year, if ever, the preacher says that it's not okay, who do you believe? Who or what carries the most weight? Pastor Peery or Prince? You may *say* Pastor Peery, but do your attitudes really square with what the Bible says? If they don't, or you think that the Bible doesn't really apply to now, how did you come up with what you believe?

Computer programmers have a saying—"Garbage in, garbage out." That is, if you load a computer with erroneous information, you will mess up the whole program—it will be worthless. To really use a computer to its fullest capacity, you have got to feed it good data. Then the results will be trustworthy. Our minds are a lot like computers. How can we hope to load our minds with things contrary to

Christianity and then get good Christian responses and actions out? By constantly listening to rock music, we run the risk of unconsciously loading our minds with garbage.

So how should we listen? The extremes are to listen to everything or nothing. As usual, the best answer lies somewhere between the extremes—somewhere in the middle. The answer is to listen—but *listen selectively.* If we are willing to become selective listeners we'll still be able to enjoy rock without being perverted by bad lyrics.

The basic ingredient in selective listening is listening. Rather obvious, you say. Not so obvious as you may think. How much of what goes on around you do you listen to? If you live near an airport, do you hear, really take notice of, every plane that takes off or lands? You may have when you first moved there, but I'll bet you don't now—unless one comes in so low it sounds as though the passengers will deplane in your living room. There is sound all around us. Often we don't even realize it is there, let alone listen to it. A person who moves from the city to the country often has a hard time getting to sleep the first few nights. Why? No sound. They may have never noticed it before—because they never really listened to diesels, sirens, and such—but they notice it now. It's too quiet.

People sound goes unnoticed, unheard, as well. How many times has someone talked to you while you've been watching TV? They speak, and you respond, usually with "uh-huh" or other profound statements. But you really haven't heard them even though you spoke back, because you were not listening to them, but to the TV. When Morris the Cat comes along hawking cat food, you look at the person you've been "conversing" with and ask, "Did you say something?" We may sit in classes all day, with teachers teaching away, and not hear a thing. Listening involves more than recognizing the presence of sound. Listening means paying attention. Paying attention is not always easy, but it's usually rewarding.

Even when we think we are listening, often we are not. Most of us can hear and comprehend more words per minute than another person can speak. We use this time differential to jump ahead in our minds—forming our agreements or arguments—then come back to the person who is speaking. By that time the speaker has moved from where we quit listening into new territory. And we didn't make the trip. We may not even be aware that they turned right or left—or that they even turned—since we were miles away in our own minds. That is how we usually listen. It is not really listening. Listening means giving our full attention to what is being said. Or, in the case of rock, what is being sung.

Rock and roll, like all music, has messages. Those messages vary from song to song They may be about sex, love, cars, drugs, war, or anything else the writer feels is important. Whatever the beat and however mindless the lyrics—and some seem awfully mindless—there is still a message, something that is being communicated. From the hauntingly beautiful "Words Get in the Way" by Miami Sound Machine, to the classic craziness of Sam the Sham and the Pharaohs' "Wooly Bully," something is being said. What it is isn't always obvious. Often we would not hear it if it was, because we don't *listen*. While we're "on hold" on the phone, the whispers of today's latest hits swing subtly over the phone lines. We bop down the boulevard with "blasters" or "boxes" balanced on our shoulders, while rapping with our friends. The seemingly ageless Dick Clark introduces the song that's got the country by the ear, and we concentrate on the Bandstand dancers, what they are wearing, and the "beat." We hardly ever notice the lyrics; but it's the lyrics that we need to watch out for.

It is easy to find out what a person's favorite song is; just ask him. Rarely will it be because of lyrics. Ask him what the song says and he will have to think about it, or just say "I dunno. . . ." And the beat goes on.

> "I give it an 85, Dick."
> "Why, Tommy?"
> "Well, it's got a good beat and it's easy to dance to."
> "Thanks, Tom. We'd like to give you the following prizes for appearing on 'Bandstand' today. . . ."

The beat goes on. And so do the lyrics. They sit there like parakeets, perched in the back of our minds, ready to fly around freely when Casey Kasem announces, "And now, the number one song on American Top 40 for the week ending. . . ." That is why we need to listen.

Parakeets are pretty birds. Parakeets sing pretty songs. But parakeets flying around in a house make pretty big messes, often pretty unpleasant ones. We want to enjoy parakeets, and not clean up messes, so we keep them in cages. We keep them under control. That way they can still play on their little birdie Ferris wheels and sing pretty songs and fly around. But they can't destroy a room.

We need to exercise the same caution with rock. If we leave our minds wide open, we can be sure that the rock birds will foul the house. And rock has some pretty big birds with nasty manners. Cleaning up is work. It is a lot easier not to allow the mess to be made in the first place.

Selective listening is the bird cage for rock. Rock can still be enjoyed without the listener being destroyed. Being a selective listener means becoming careful about what you listen to. Becoming discriminating. Mature. You are, after all, an individual with individual tastes. Become refined in your musical tastes, as well. You wouldn't buy every pair of jeans that Levi's makes just because Levi's makes them, would you? Why listen to every kind of song on the radio just because it's by Journey?

Use song titles to cue you in to what's coming lyrically. When the announcer cues "Mandolin Rain" you can be reasonably sure it's not about getting it on in the back of Dad's Olds. Likewise, a song with a title like "If Loving You Is Wrong, I Don't Want to Be Right" probably isn't going to be on the list approved by the Bureau of Christian Standards and Ethics. Titles offer only clues, though. You still have to listen to the lyrics.

Tight harmonies and slick production aren't marks of safety either. Atlantic Starr's "Secret Lovers" is awfully pretty—until you listen to the lyrics. Then you realize it's pretty awful. The song is fairly overt in its message, and the message is contrary to Christianity. We often find ourselves sucked in by innocent-sounding arrangements or a driving beat. Once in, it's hard to get out. Remember, it's not the melody or back beat that pollutes the mind—it's the lyrics.

Paying attention is work. It takes more effort than many of us care to expend. For some reason it doesn't come naturally. But paying attention is the only safe and sane way to enjoy rock as a Christian. Compromise with the world should not be an option. So pay attention we must.

Take a few minutes now. Go turn on a radio or record player, or slip in a tape. Listen to a song—any song—carefully. Really listen.

Now that you're back, a few questions: What did the song say? Do you agree? Why or why not? Get a piece of paper and jot down your answers. Feels like homework, doesn't it? Now, try to sum up the song's message in ten words or less. Determine what it really is about. Why does the singer feel that it is important to take up your time with this song? Is the message commercial (something just to sell a song) or does it have merit?

Look at what you have written. All about one song and how it affects you. Now multiply this by the number of songs you listen to in a day. The effect they have is staggering—and we often don't realize it.

Other questions follow this exercise. What's going to be your response to this song from now on, now that you've examined the song? Will you listen to it again? Can you hear it over and over and not let it affect you?

Sometimes it's hard to know what the lyrics mean. Sometimes the meaning is obvious, sometimes it seems to be buried. Usually it's in the open. Yet people constantly search for the deeper meanings in rock. They ignore students of rock, like Jann Wenner, founder of *Rolling Stone* magazine, who says, "It's primarily not an intellectual thing. It's music, that's all."[2] And so it is. But the search still goes on.

A few years back a person writing on the contemporary scene said that "Puff the Magic Dragon" was about the joys of drug use. If you listened carefully, the writer said, you knew that what was really being said was that you should "puff the magic drag in"—that is, inhale the smoke from a marijuana cigarette. People were stunned to learn this. "Puff" was one of the top ten songs in the spring of 1963. The pretty melody, coupled with a seemingly cute story and pleasing three-part harmony, made the song a hit. Millions of people bought the record and taught it to their children. Then they found out it was about drugs. They were devastated.

So were the song's writers. One of them, Peter Yarrow (Peter of Peter, Paul, and Mary), denied that it was about drugs. While on a recent "reunion tour" with Paul and Mary, he talked of how a person could make any song a drug song by searching for hidden meanings. To explain his point he used "The Star Spangled Banner."

"Oh, say can you see?" (See=C, which stands for cocaine)
"By the dawn's early light" (the time when junkies shoot up)

and on and on. Francis Scott Key would be appalled to think that people had labeled his song a covert drug culture song. Of course it isn't, any more than "Puff the Magic Dragon" is.

Top 40 messages are rarely hidden. You won't have to spend lots of time trying to uncover the secret truths encoded in the lyrics. They simply aren't there. If you think they are, that's okay with the record companies. If that gets you to buy the album in order to listen for the meanings, great. The real message they have for you is, "We want your money."

Another form of hidden messages supposedly going on is known as backmasking. Backmasking is when a group lays down a track that can only be heard when the record is played backward. The first charges of backmasking were brought against the Beatles. "Revolution 9" on *The White Album* has a voice that repeats "number nine, number nine," which, when played backward, supposedly says, "turn me on, dead man," referring, said those in the know, to the "premature death" of Beatle Paul McCartney. Another space, played backward, is supposed to say, "Paul is dead, miss him, miss him." While the Beatles denied both that they used backmasking or that Paul was dead, fans bought the records, looking for these (and other) hidden, backward messages. And the money rolled in.

Backward masking can be done. The Beatles did try a little, usually backmasking an instrumental, not vocal, part.

Other groups have done it as well. But from an artist's point of view, it is a detriment. The object of recording is to obtain as clear and crisp a sound as possible. Backmasking just muddies the sound. It is also expensive. So a lot of backmasking is a gimmick—something to get the consumer to buy the product. Since radio stations aren't going to play the record backward—their time is too valuable to them to mess around with such silliness—if you want to find out if there is a hidden message, you'll have to buy the record. That's what the record companies want.

The messages are not all as terrible as we have been told, either. While some antirock folks show how all messages are satanic, the fact is that they're not. In one of the most recent examples, the group Styx included some backmasking on their 1983 release "Kilroy Was Here." If we play the record backward, we hear an ominous voice repeating what seems to be a chant in some strange foreign tongue. The words? *Annuit Coeptis* and *Novus Ordo Seclorum.* The language? Latin. Their meaning? The first means "He [God] has favored our undertakings." The second says "A new order of the Ages." Where can you find them? Open your wallet and pull out a dollar bill. Look at the Great Seal of the United States of America. That's where the words come from, and they refer to the founding of our nation. Styx is obviously poking fun at those looking for secret, hidden backward messages.

The danger from these backward messages has been exaggerated. It is extremely doubtful that the mind can unravel these backward words. Even if it could, why would they be more evil or have more satanic power than the words going by frontwards? Hidden messages are not nearly as dangerous as the obvious ones—the ones that speakers spew forth constantly. You have to listen carefully. Only by doing so can you decide whether or not you buy that message. If you don't pay attention, you will probably buy it without even knowing it.

There are many songs that don't deserve airplay. Or home play. Once again, I want to stress that I mean lyrics, not back beat or melody. Style is a matter of taste—it's subjective. Taste is why some people love a song that others can't stand. All of us can tell, though, whether a song's message is worth listening to or not. The equipment for making such decisions is standard on all humans—two ears and the gray stuff that lies between them. Use the computer that God gave you. Lead the song in and see how it fits into your programming. If the bell rings, sirens wail, and the IBM under your hair prints out, "Garbage!" then behave accordingly. Shut it off or change the station. That takes courage. I say courage because as soon as you do it, one of your tried and true friends will yelp, "Whadidyagoandodatfor? That's my favorite song!" So you'll either have to change it back, or—and here is where you need courage—explain why you changed it. To say you don't like it won't be enough. Your friends will want to know why. Becoming a selective listener means you may face some ridicule. But anything worth believing is worth standing up for.

Being a selective listener brings benefits other than just being able to listen to rock. We are called to be witnesses. Usually we are afraid. After all, we're no Moses, though he didn't seem to think he was much of a public speaker, either, as I recall. Standing on soapboxes on downtown street corners isn't our style. "I don't know what to say," is our common refrain. And it's true. We don't know what to say. We want to say *something,* to help people in need, but feel inadequate, stupid, ashamed, and incompetent. We feel human.

Careful listening to rock music can make you aware of human needs you can meet in Christ's name. These needs are both local and worldwide. Quincy Jones's all-star production of "We Are the World" reminds us vividly of the needs of starving children. True, we don't know whether or not Jones is operating from a Christian perspective. But as noted musician/songwriter Noel Stookey says, all good music, all music that directs our thoughts to that which is beyond ourselves, comes from the Holy Spirit, whether the artist knows it or not. All *good* things come from God. And Jesus told us to feed the hungry. "We Are the World" reminds us, if we let it, of that command. And being so reminded, we can reach out by donating our Cherry-Coke-and-burger money to World Vision or some other worthy agency. Then people with full physical tummies will be ready to feed their spiritual tummies with the Bread of Life.

The need for peace—and not just ending "The War"—was forced into us in the sixties and seventies by songs like "Wake Up, Everybody" and "Your Flag Decal Won't Get You Into Heaven Anymore." We Christians had our eyes opened to Jesus' command to be peacemakers—making peace in our homes, schools, offices, cities, nations, and world. We searched the Scriptures and found that peacemaking was active, something we did, not passive. Peacemaking meant writing letters to government officials explaining our religious stands, stands that are often unpopular. But then Jesus has not called us to a popularity contest. He has called us to discipleship. We are called to place His kingdom over ours. Biblical peacemakers did not respond out of naive political dreams, but out of obedience. The times rolled on, the war wound down, and many radical protesters became stockbrokers or insurance salesmen and moved to the suburbs. Their commitment to peace faded with the sunset, leaving the biblical peacemakers to carry on. And they did, even when no one seemed to notice. The songs reminded us that peace was needed. They put fire in our hearts to make a difference. God's Spirit placed it in our bones and drove us on.

While we are concerned with the world at large, usually the part that concerns us the most is our daily existence, our homes and family. Rock reminds us that most of us live in a world that is largely mundane, seemingly without purpose. One rock writer lifts a classic literary phrase when he sings about, "lives of quiet desperation." We see people like that every day. All of us know folks who are lonely, depressed, or worse. When you hear Madonna pleading "Papa Don't Preach," you can't help but be reminded of friends who may be in that situation.

Something as simple as a smile can communicate God's love. Helping someone does not mean that you cart a 120-pound Bible around and tell them, "God loves you and so do I." No. It means showing you care, being available to listen. Jesus is our example. He always had time for people. As His follower, just listen to the Holy Spirit. He will direct you in doing the right things. They will come naturally.

If you have ever moved to a new school and had to make friends, you know what it is to be lonely. Sadly enough, there are people who live their whole lives that way. It is as if they had fallen off a bicycle and are afraid to get back on. They don't want to get hurt. You can help get them back on the cycle of friendship. You may be afraid, too. By sharing that, and the love of a God who never forsakes, you can make a difference in their lives. You can help someone who looks at life tentatively become someone who really enjoys life, because he has met the Giver of all life—God. And he has met Him through you.

Hunger, peace, loneliness are just a few of the problems people face. There are many more. Rock shouts out the needs. It is a contemporary form of expression. If you are a selective listener, it can sensitize you to people around you. It can open doors of ministry for you.

Being a good listener means being a careful one. So listen—really listen—to the music. Dare to be different, to change stations or shut the stuff off. Ask what it says, and why. Then look around, see people in need, and go make a difference in the world. You can, you know. All you have to do is try.

---

1. Steve Clapp, *Teenage Sexuality: A Crisis and an Opportunity for the Church* (Sidell, Ill.: C-4 Publications, 1981), p. 4.

2. Dave Marsh and Kevin Stein, *The Book of Rock Lists* (New York: Dell Publishing Company, Inc., 1981), p. 8.

7
Rock and Roll Relief
(for Parents)

If the last chapter could have been "How Should We Listen?" this one could be "How Should We Put Up With It?" Chapter 6 was mostly for the young'uns—those doing the listening. This is for those who must endure that about which Mitch Miller said, "It's not music, it's a disease."[1] There are many who would agree with Miller. Like disease, rock is highly contagious. It has swept through the teen and preteen population for three decades. A sort of musical bubonic plague. Symptoms start with talking about favorite stars and their songs. You know your teen is in advanced stages when you hop into the family car after Junior's had it out, turn the key, and give the car a sunroof when you are hurtled through the top by the total wattage of the car radio tuned to a rock station.

There is hope—and it comes not from doctors, but rather from a rock star. Jackson Browne admits in his song "Daddy's Tune" that ol' Dad is a tad more on the ball than previously thought. Just as Mark Twain imparted hope to parents of his day when he wrote how amazed he was at how much his father had learned by the time Twain reached twenty-one, so should Browne offer hope to parents of today. It is sad that the teen years are often as hard on the parents as on their progeny. But recognition of parental love, concern, and intelligence does come. The secret of its coming sooner rather than later belongs to those parents who have learned to keep lines of communication open. That's not easy. With communication, though, comes respect and—best of all—love.

This chapter is in many ways more about communication than about rock and roll. Rock isn't the disease, it is only a symptom. Adolescence is the disease. Communication is one of the cures.

Communication is important. A simple statement, but often ignored or taken for granted. It is much too important to be treated that way. We are living in an age of information. We would not be if the means to communicate were not present. More and more companies are giving their employees courses in communication. When big business says something is important, our society takes it seriously. Yet, in one of the most important places—the family—communication often breaks down.

Parents are concerned about communication. They should be. I encourage you to seek out books like Norman Wakefield's *Listening: A Christian Guide to Loving Relationships* and *Between Parent and Teenager* by Dr. Haim Ginott. These books give insights on healthy relationships and handles on the fine art of communication. They teach us how to be good communicators, including—listeners. And they are practical. Their ideas are more than theory, they work.

Encouraging selective listening in teens is the primary thrust of this book. Using it as a communication bridge in the family is the direction of this chapter. To get started, listed below you will find a few general listening tips. They deal mostly with conversation, but can also be used in selective listening.

First, *listen for themes*. Teens, like everybody else, talk about the things that matter to them. Those things may seem to be unimportant to us. The latest gear ratio on a new Corvette or Suzi's brother's girl friend's new perm may seem inconsequential. Listen anyhow. That says, "I find what you think important." If you really want to surprise them, learn something about their favorite subject and *you* introduce it into the conversation. Taking such an interest shows that you are interested in their lives. Listening for themes enables you to be aware of what's on their minds.

Second, *listen for feelings.* This is harder than listening for themes. Feelings are often covered up with piles of seemingly meaningless trivia. Talk that comes out as anger may be a disguise for feelings of pain or rejection. JoAnn may be mad at LuAnn for not inviting her to a party, but is she really mad . . . or hurt? Your helping, or hurting, the situation depends largely on your ability to listen for feelings.

Third, *listen for information.* When Tom comes home from school and rattles off an endless list of names, dates, and places—pay attention. Pay attention, that is, if you want to know where he is at ten-thirty on Friday night. A good bit of frustration and trouble can be avoided by listening to information. You can be sure that as soon as you say, "I didn't know that," Tom will say, "I told you last Thursday." He probably did.

These three basics should help you in the struggle to keep lines open. If you show that you are willing to listen, then you have already won a major victory.

Back to rock. More good news. There is yet more hope for parents weary of shouting, "Turn that noise down," or walking around with ears full of cotton. Loudness is a phase.

The taillights of the old Chevy had barely winked out of sight when I decided to crank the stereo up. It was one of those rare nights when my parents and my three little sisters had gone somewhere and I didn't have to go. I was seventeen. I had awaited this night with glee, specially selecting the discs that were to be my transport to hi-fi heaven. With the Beatles I went to "Penny Lane." Buffalo Springfield told me that "Somethin's Happenin' Here." And then the phone rang. A voice with an edge on it like Jack the Ripper's knife informed me that if I didn't turn "that noise down" I would be lucky to live till my next birthday. I never asked who was calling, but I didn't doubt the sincerity of the sentiment. I quietly replaced the receiver, tiptoed over to the stereo and clicked it off, and hid under the sofa until found there later by my folks, who thought I was playing Charades and variously guessed "bowl of Jell-O," *Murder at the Rue Morgue*, and others. Though I have played records loudly since (never in that neighborhood, however), I've never let it reach a level where I had to fear instant death coming over the phone lines.

Times change. Now *I* make the calls—mostly to the kid down the street who plays his stereo so loudly I can hear it over my Lawn Boy. To be truthful, I haven't really called. I would never inflict such psychic pain on anyone—even if I wanted to. Besides, I just don't have the sort of voice that instills fear. But, if you happen to be reading this, Kid in the yellow house, turn that racket down.

Parents, try to remember that loudness is a rite of passage. Don't be afraid to ask the kids to turn it down. An honest, politely phrased, nonsarcastic request can achieve results. Pained expressions or direct military orders achieve results, too, but they're usually short of pleasant. Are you willing to pay the cost?

A cost you might be willing to pay is for a set of headphones. The use of headphones enables the listener to enjoy his or her music and the rest of their family their peace. In other words, the rocker can go ahead and destroy his or her eardrums, while the family china remains intact. Think about it.

Another way to cope with kids and rock is to get nostalgic. Climb up in the attic, or down in the crawl space, dust off the old trunk, get out the high school yearbooks, and play some of the golden oldies you have saved. Relive the good old days and remember *your* parents' reactions to your music and antics. While few parents of today's teens had records that came on 78s, those of you who did remember, if you will, classics like Spike Jones' "William Tell Overture" or "Marzy Doats." Teens from the fifties can recall poetic masterpieces such as "Alley Oop" and "Tutti Frutti." To be sure "Alley Oop" is not representative of all fifties rock, there were some real deep songs like "Jingle Bell Rock." The point is, how did your folks react to Sam Cooke's "You Send Me"? Did they love it—or did they want to send *you*?

If your parents were supportive of you, even if they didn't understand you, be that way with your kids. That doesn't mean you "ooh" and "aah" over every new song. Your parents didn't, and your kids wouldn't like it if you did. There is something phony about an adult, especially a parent, trying to be "with it." It's embarrassing. Your kids are not looking for you to be their best friend. They have friends already. What they want, and need, is a parent. They want someone who cares about them and their world, but they don't need you to act like an overgrown teen.

Take an interest in what your teens are involved with. That is not always easy. My older son, Ben, had an addiction to *Star Wars* sound tracks. They left me cold. But hour after hour, on long, cold winter evenings, the London Symphony sounded forth from his room as he built Lego starships and saved the universe from the forces of evil.

This could have been irritating. Or I could have appreciate his love of music (after all, *my* parents like his taste more than my taste), talked with him about it, and reached a sound level that is agreeable to both of us. I could have *ordered* him to turn it down—or off. I am the Parent. But why risk breaking a nine-year-old's heart when something in between would satisfy? What purpose would that have served? By talking about it, we both ended up happy. Ben got to save the universe, and I got to read the funnies in peace. Now that he's a teen, we listen to Huey Lewis and the News together.

If your folks were intolerant and made you feel like a worm, think back to all the times you said, "Well, when I'm a parent, I'll never treat my kid like that." Then be the kind of parent *you* wanted. That is difficult. Usually the only parenting course we ever took was from our parents, watching them parent us. It takes more formal education to get a driver's license than to become a parent. We learn all the time, usually by observing. So, if you had rotten parents, and want to learn new ways, get yourself some books on Christian parenting. Then remember the way your parents treated you and your vows. Remember, remember, remember.

Yet another, and really the best, way to put up with rock is to be a supporter of selective listening. Granted, most parents' ideal of selective listening is to shut off, but that is not realistic. It probably won't happen by itself, and if you make it happen you will have to deal with feelings of anger and hostility.

Being a parent is not the same as being an animal trainer; though a friend of mine often refers to human young as "rug rats" or "yard apes." The hospital does not issue whips and chairs to the parents of each newborn. We may often feel that being a parent is a lot like walking into a cage and sticking our heads in the lion's mouth. It is not. We are not in the business of intimidating children into "appropriate" behavior We are not trainers of lions and tigers. If that is how we operate, we had best pray that the glue in the chair holds and the whip retains its sting. The day the chair falls apart or the whip is out of reach, we will be eaten alive— usually by having our hearts broken. And we will wonder why.

So while ordering that music off may be effective from the parental standpoint, it is not the answer. Encouraging selective listening is. That is because it shows our kids that, even though we may not like it, we realize it is important to them.

My wife, Sharon, has some dearly held beliefs regarding food. Nutrition is a necessity. The day that a steaming portion of cauliflower was placed before Ben, I felt my body wracked with cold chills. I was sure he wouldn't eat it. After all, it's good for him. Braced as I was for "what's this stuff" and "I don't care if it is good for me, I won't eat it" (spoken in the dialect of a then three-year-old), I was surprised. He ate it. He had realized how important this funny-looking stuff was to his mother. Because of his willingness to indulge one of his mother's quirks, peace and tranquillity reigned. Mother was pleased, my digestive tract returned to normal, and Ben emerged unscathed. He also found his mother willing to accommodate some of his wishes. The kid is no fool. He's smarter than I am—I still drop the cauliflower into the napkin on my lap and sneak it to the trash pail. And get caught.

Another advantage to Ben's eating his cauliflower is he found out that he liked it. It opened up a whole new dimension of culinary delights. He still prefers cake and cookies to cauliflower. But that's okay; he has expanded his horizons and has grown—physically and other ways—because of it.

Encouraging selective listening may do for you what Ben's experiment with cauliflower did for him. You'll certainly show your teens that you recognize their music's importance to them. And you may find that not all styles of rock are as bad as you had thought. You might even like some. Of course, you will probably still prefer Montovani to Van Halen. That's okay. Just try these new "vegetables" with an open mind. After all, we are most alive when we are unafraid of growing and trying new things.

Another benefit is that we will be able to hear what is on the minds of young people. We want to know what's going on in our youngsters' lives, but we spend too much time wringing our hands and moaning about a generation gap. Bridging the gap is easier if we listen to and respect the themes sung about. If you are sensitive to your issues being valued, value theirs. People who share common concerns tend to share other things, too—things like love and trust.

You may also find that, because of your initiative and trust, your kids will be more selective, and quieter. The home battle zone will fade as conflicts, in the area of music, cease. Your fairness encourages them to be fair. A welcome side effect is that what comes out of the stereo will be less objectionable.

As a teen, rainy days usually found my buddies and me playing cards at Mike Rader's. Mike's dad had been in the navy in World War II and had brought home a deck of cards with silhouettes of American and Japanese warplanes on them. Each card had its own picture, nickname, and the caption "Know Your Enemy." We played with these cards so much that if a Zeke or a Betty swooped in over the rooftops today, I would still dive for cover.

Knowing our enemies is important. Sometimes we find that they aren't enemies at all, just someone or something we have not understood. Just like the neighborhood bully who is feared until the littlest runt on the street stands up to him and everyone sees the bully's loneliness and insecurities, we can discover that our enemies are not all as tough or bad as we had thought. With some friendliness they might even become our friends. This is true of rock. Though conditioned by Christian antirockers such as David A. Noebel to see "the evil vortex of rock 'n' roll and its subculture,"[2] if we really look for it, we find it's not any greater there than in the world of advertising or stockbrokering. It is not any worse, or any better, than most segments of today's society. It is difficult to imagine Kerry Livgren, Kansas, Rick Cua of the Outlaws, U2, and other avowed Christians participating in something that is beyond God's grace. Rock is not the enemy we have been told it is.

Test it for yourself. Listen to some. *Gasp, he's got to be kidding!* Think about it. How will you know what you're talking about if you've never heard it? Your arguments against it aren't yours—they are someone else's unless you've listened for yourself. Much "information" about rock is based on rumor and innuendo. People, sometimes good Christian people, are often dredging up hidden messages and symbols that simply aren't there. So listen to the music. See if *you* discover any hidden messages. Remember, rock is rarely subtle; meanings are out in the open. This also prevents your kids from putting something over on you since you'll already know what the songs are about.

Listening opens up pathways for dialogue. Talk with your kids about the songs you have heard. After they get over the shock of *you* listening to *their* music, you'll find new opportunities for discussion. Listening together also opens avenues of communication that may have been closed for repair. Listening/dialogue helps you find areas of mutual concern: the new immorality, the world situation, modern life, and so on. We often feel that communication between the generations is difficult because each has different interests. That's not usually the case. It's not the interests that are so different, but rather the means of expressing them. The language is different. Many adults feel that Adolescent English should be taught as a foreign language. Closing the gap by selective listening allows each side to hear the other without using an Adult/Teenagese dictionary. Listening together shows concern and caring on the part of the adult that the teen won't expect. It does, that is, if the intent is true dialogue and not to put down rock. The listening will also be unproductive if it's done out of a sense of duty. Teenagers may have a lot to learn, but they can spot someone who is only playing a game. And they won't play along. If your concern is real, selective listening could be one of your closest family times.

"Okay," you say, "how do I start? I don't know where to begin." The first place to look is in the back of this book. Use some of the discussion starters listed there. They are general ones and will have to be molded to particular songs, but they are a beginning.

Another good source is *Group* magazine (Thom Schultz Publications, P.O. Box 481, Loveland, CO 80539). *Group* is an interdenominational magazine published for young people and their leaders. A regular feature is a section called "Top 40." "Top 40" is a discussion guide using songs from *Billboard*'s Hot 100, the hundred hits getting the most airplay and sales. The column includes Scripture passages and questions for each song. While they are meant to be used with a youth group, they can be easily adapted for individual use. Each issue of *Group* has a "Top 40" on two songs. A sample "Top 40" column is included below.

She Works Hard for the Money
DONNA SUMMER

Have your kids listen closely to the record, trying to figure out what the person does who "works hard for the money." Then let them know that Summer wrote this song about a woman who works as an attendant in a women's rest room.

Ask them to think about their own future jobs. Would they like or hate a job like the woman in the song has? What are the career plans of those in the room? List their vocational choices on a blackboard or large sheet of paper. Ask how they decided on that occupation—money, parents' wishes, prestige, or what? Read 1 Corinthians 7:17; Ephesians 4:1; and 2 Timothy 1:8–9. Does God have certain jobs in store for everyone? How do we know what it is he wants us to do? Is work that a Christian does really a vocation—a calling? Explain.

Close by reading Romans 12:1–2 in unison.

The hardest part of selective listening as a family is finding time. All of us are busy and getting everyone together at one time in one place is difficult. But the mere notion of listening to rock as a family is so novel that it may be all you need to keep the younger set home. They will want to see what you've got up your sleeve.

To set it in motion, just ask them if they would like to listen to some records. Make sure they know you mean theirs, not yours. When they come to, situate yourselves near a music maker and listen. Listen carefully, analyzing what you are hearing. What is the song saying? Why do you think it's saying that? Is it important? In other words, do the same things the last chapter taught the kids to do. The only difference will be the value judgments you each bring. The teens will have their age group's perspective and prejudices, and you'll have yours. Try to convince everyone to be open.

Take time to really communicate. This takes work. You will have to do some homework, getting ready for discussion time. Be open and candid. Don't be afraid to admit that you don't have all the answers. Kids need to know that their folks are human and have questions, too. They also need to know that their folks realize their own humanity. Try to remember what it was like to be a kid. Too often we get bogged down in our woes and forget that kids' problems are as real and valid as our own. They deserve to be listened to. Having a family listening time shows that you honor their tastes and are willing to try to understand them.

You've got to be genuine. None of this will work if it is seen as a gimmick or the old folks just trying to be cool. Trust and love must be developed. Keeping the feelings flowing means taking a risk and revealing your own feelings.

How long has it been since you told your kid, "I love you"? Not, "I love you, but I wish you'd clean up your room," or, "I love you, but get your feet off the coffee table." Just, "I love you." You may have to demonstrate your love by admitting you've made mistakes and need forgiveness—both from your teen and Christ. Far too often we parent along our merry way, calling on God only when situations become unbearable. The Lord of our lives wants to be included every step of our way. Reintroduce Him to your family by beginning your listening time with prayer. Allow these times to help make you a better parent.

The teen years are tremendously difficult. They always have been, but today they're even harder. Kids find themselves adrift on a sea of conflicting ideas—parents say this, peers say that, school says something else. Lines of communication have frayed and fallen. It is the wise parent indeed who can keep the lines up and open. The best way is to just be there, available. That doesn't ensure communication, but it demonstrates that two important ingredients—love and trust—are present. People today need love, and they search until they find it. Society shows love by the gifts lavished. Diamonds, clothes, TVs, cars, and more. It neglects the most important gift—time. Taking time to play, eat, or listen to records together shows someone he is important. Feeling important to someone makes me feel good about myself. I'll bet it does you, too.

Parenting has never been easy. It never will be. Keeping communication flowing is aided by making room for their 45s beside your 78s.

Loving is the only way to survive.

---

1. Dave Marsh and Kevin Stein, *The Book of Rock Lists* (New York: Dell Publishing Company, Inc., 1981), p. 7.
2. Book Review Section, *Contemporary Christian Music* (June 1983), p. 29.

8

Regenerated Rock

In the 1970s pop recording star Chris Christian asked the musical question "Why does the devil have all the good music?" Good question. Sometimes it seems that he does. Otherwise we wouldn't have to be so careful about what we listen to. The way sex is used and abused in rock is just one example. We know that God approves of sex—after all, He created it. But we also know that He didn't mean it to be portrayed as it often is in rock. Rock-and-roll sex is usually incomplete. Sex is shown as a mere physical act. And though much of our modern world would like us to believe that it is, it isn't. God means it to be more, but the music perverts it. Then it's no longer God's—and the music isn't either. But as we talked about earlier, the selling of sex in song is just one example of secular rock's sleazy side.

Of course, selective listening is one answer. Being a selective listener isn't always easy though. It demands concentration and effort, two things we often try to avoid if we can. Since the music itself—the back beat, bass, and screaming guitars—is okay and all we want to avoid is raunchy lyrics, we wonder if there is any way to relax and enjoy good old rock and roll short of buying only instrumental discs. Well, kind of.

Christian's question about the devil having all the good music is a gross oversimplification of the subject—as well as a huge exaggeration (as opposed to a little exaggeration such as, "If I told you once, I've told you six times . . ."). The devil doesn't have it all. In fact much of humankind's best stuff, the really great music, has been dedicated to the worship of God. But Christian isn't singing his question to a panel of classical musicians or church organists. Instead he's singing to rockers like himself. Like you. And, as I've already said, it does sometimes seem as if the devil has it all—if by "good" music you mean rock. (And if you've read this far, that probably is your definition of good music.) I'll bet that Christian isn't asking about a good moral over a bad one either; he's talking about good melody, good performing, and good production, too. ("It's got a great beat. I give it a 95, Dick.") Rock has often seemed to be the devil's domain (and some would leave it there), with the good becoming harder and harder to find.

That's not true any longer. The past few years have brought us born-again rock and rollers, playing everything from southern-fried gospel to new wave and heavy metal. These bands and individuals bring good rock to a world hungry for good music and a good word. Unlike many of their contemporaries, their songs are not sex-saturated or drug-induced. Like their fellow rockers they are regularly on the charts, played on major rock stations, and fill concert halls with loyal fans who have come to hear rock without having to worry about the words.

In the early eighties there were several Christian artists on the charts receiving extensive airplay—from "Do Right" by Paul Davis to U2's "(Pride) In the Name of Love." One kid I spoke to was floored to learn that most of the members of U2 were Christians. "That's hard to believe," he said. "Why?" I asked. "Because they're *good.*" And they are. All the way around. Musically, lyrically, performingly. Our secular society needs to be penetrated by such committed Christian artists if we want to reach the world with the good news of Jesus Christ.

This trend is continuing. Probably the best-known Christian rock and roller is Amy Grant. Starting out as a young teen (she signed her first recording contract at age fifteen and recorded her first album at seventeen), Amy has become probably the best-known Christian artist. Her *Age to Age* was the first Christian album by a soloist to go platinum. She regularly tours and fills some of the most prestigious concert halls in America. Her songs have been near the top on all the charts—Christian and *Billboard's* "Hot 100." Her videos have been on MTV. She's recorded chart-stopping duets with the likes of Peter Cetera, the former lead singer of Chicago. She's taking a wholesome Christian message where one needs to be heard—to secular radio.

That's important. And she told *People* magazine, "It's like there's a huge mountain called the music business, and this thing next to it, a little bitty saltshaker—that's the Christian music business. My question is, how can I sing to that mountain of people out there?"

What she's gotten for trying to sing to that mountain is a lot of grief, mostly from Christians who think other Christians should sing only "Christian songs" in "Christian locations." Fortunately for Amy, she's done what she feels God would have her do instead of what some of her Christian fans think she should do. And because of her willingness to be on the cutting edge of contemporary music, she's bringing the gospel to people who would never enter a church. They buy her albums and find a refreshing difference from much of rock—a difference that talks about love and friendship and life the way God meant it to be. And if there is any doubt as to the source of her music, the listener has merely to look at the record jacket and the Scripture verses printed there. Thanks to Amy, and others like her, there is cause for rejoicing even on regular rock stations.

Besides these born-again types on the Top 40 there is a whole other kind of religious rocker. That one's music comes under the umbrella of what is called Contemporary Christian Music. It's an outgrowth of the old gospel music and the Jesus People movement of the seventies.

Gospel music has been around a long time. Pretty much an American phenomenon, gospel used to mean four fellows and their pianist. It was sung in four-part harmony. Every town had a gospel group that sang in the local churches. As their fame spread to the surrounding counties and states, they would cut a custom record of their harmonizing on the old gospel standards ("Will There Be Any Stars in My Crown" and "Gospel Ship"), buy an old bus, and travel a bit more widely. They sang for love offerings (or "free will" offerings) and a chance to sell their records. A part-time ministry by the otherwise full-time employed, it made little money. And went largely unnoticed, except by the locals.

Gospel groups are still around—and still largely unnoticed save for friends and family. Gospel, though, is bigger than ever. Last year, that segment of the recording industry known as gospel captured 6 percent of the total dollars Americans spent on recorded products. That's over $210 million, just for records, CDs, and tapes. That figure does not include concerts, songbooks, or any other related items. Why the big change? It's because gospel now has a component known as CCM—Contemporary Christian Music.

CCM has come a long way in a few years. From a handful of middle-of-the-road pop releases (like Ralph Carmichael's "My Front Porch") and off-the-garage-wall-sounding records ("The Everlastin' Living Jesus Music Concert"), to offerings in any format desired, new wave to Christian country-western, CCM has burst on the collective consciousness of Christians like a firecracker on the Fourth of July. Even K mart sells it. ("Attention K mart shoppers, we have a blue light special on CCM at register five.") *Billboard*, the magazine of the music and entertainment business, gives it almost weekly news coverage and has a reporter (Bob Darden) and column ("Lecturn") on it as well as charts of the biggest records. Magazines like *Contemporary Christian Music* and *Musicline* are devoted almost exclusively to CCM. Most other Christian magazines regularly review new releases. There is even an equivalent of MTV (CCMTV?) being talked about.

But it wasn't always like this. CCM grew out of the Jesus music of the Jesus Movement of the late sixties and early seventies. The Jesus Movement was reaching a generation raised on TV and rock and roll. It began when the Christian World Liberation Front opened in the infamous Haight-Ashbury area near the University of California. It was probably the first Christian coffee house dedicated to spreading the gospel message to non-Christian, nonchurch-going, college-age folks. It was successful in its outreach and others followed across the country. Another phenomenon of the Jesus Movement was the distribution of "Jesus papers." They were modeled on the popular "underground" papers that circulated around college campuses and were not governed by the faculty or administration. In many ways, the Jesus Movement took the radical energy of the day, with all its trappings, and repackaged it. Instead of questions being raised, though, it was questions being answered.

One of the most popular aspects of the Jesus Movement was the music. It was hard-driving, radical rock and roll or mellowed-out folk rock, all presented with a Christian message. And wherever the Jesus Movement went, Jesus music went as well. Those who heard it, liked it—or at least most of it. The old hymns of the church and southern gospel, while okay, didn't really do anything for them. Up until that time those were the only choices. Those who wanted inspiration had to choose between rock and religion, for never had the twain met before. Then came the Jesus music. Larry Norman, echoing the sentiments of the Jesus People and other young Christians, musically asked, "Why should the devil have all the good music?" Then decided he shouldn't and started the musical explosion that has become CCM.

Norman and his albums *Upon this Rock*, *Street Level*, and *Bootleg* paved the way for today's CCM. Norman had been in rock groups since he was a teenager, and he and his band People even gave Capitol Records a number 14 on the national charts with their 1968 hit "I Love You (But the Words Won't Come)." Norman was a Christian and left the band the day that their first album was released, feeling that the commercial nature of secular rock and roll would stifle his freedom to sing about Jesus. A year later he recorded his first solo album, *Upon this Rock*, for Capitol. It was the first nationally distributed, major-label Jesus-music album.

Calvary Chapel of Costa Mesa, California, set up Maranatha! ("The Lord Cometh") music in 1971. They put out all sorts of sounds to help disseminate this joyous Jesus music. Other companies, like Bob Cottrell's Creative Sound, distributed early Jesus rock, including some of Maranatha! Music's, since there were no national organizations to get the word out.

Jesus-music radio stations began to spring up. Scott Ross, a former New York City deejay, helped set up the first "gospel rock" radio show in 1969, on Pat Robertson's fledgling CBN radio network. Sixteen radio stations were on line by early 1970, with more showing enthusiastic interest. Soon there were 175 stations nationwide broadcasting "The Scott Ross Show."

Though Scott Ross is probably the best known of the

early Jesus music deejays, others soon followed. One was Paul Baker, who developed the "Sounds Like . . ." chart in the back of this book. In 1970 he began broadcasting another nationally syndicated show, "A Joyful Noise." Finally, in 1975, the first all-Jesus-music radio station went on the air. Now most major radio markets have at least one station whose format is based on CCM releases.

In the early seventies even secular recording companies got in on the act, figuring that if kids were buying Jesus rock by unknown artists, perhaps there was a market for them. Ray Steven's "Everything Is Beautiful," with an opening that featured a chorus of kids singing "Jesus Loves the Little Children," went to number 1 on *Billboard*'s charts in 1970. Judy Collins's rendition of "Amazing Grace" went to 15. Country-pop star Glen Campbell made it onto the charts with "I Knew Jesus (Before He Was a Star)." Even Sha-Na-Na, the nostalgia doo-wop group formed originally of students from Columbia University, hit the Hot 100 with a parody of all the Jesus rock songs—"Are You on the Top 40 (Of Your Lordy, Lordy, Lordy)."

Also big were rock operas like *Godspell* and *Jesus Christ Superstar*. These presentations of the gospel, though not always written by believing Christians, packed theaters and cinemas across the country.

Then the Jesus Movement began to fade from the nation's consciousness. The recording industry, always trying to find a new fad, let Jesus songs drop and went on to something else. The "One Way" sign and most other trappings of the Jesus Movement have largely faded away, but the music hasn't. It was good and it spoke to those who heard it. It still does.

Many of the acts from the early days have passed from the scene—groups like Love Song, the Armagedon Experience, and so on. Some still remain, like the 2nd Chapter of Acts and Daniel Amos, maturing with the music. Daniel

Amos, for instance, has gone from what one early reviewer said was "out-Eagling the Eagles" to being on the cutting edge of New Wave CCM. Quite a change.

The early days were hard on performers. No one really knew how to manage Jesus music. Setting up concert halls, sound systems, travel and lodging arrangements, and selling tickets was something new. In the past, gospel singers had stayed in parishioners' homes, eaten at carry-in dinners, sung in the sanctuary, and lived off the money from their day jobs. Free-will offerings generally covered the cost of getting the bus there, and record sales financed the recording of their next album. Now, with the popularity of Jesus music, groups were traveling more. Hotel rooms had to be rented—or should have been. Many times groups were caught in the bind of having inadequate sound equipment, poor ticket sales, and low attendance. All this was because no one really knew how to promote Jesus rock. Over time, people learned, but often at the expense of the performers. No one would say that people were trying to take advantage of the singers. But regardless of that, royalty checks and concert receipts were few and far between, or sometimes nonexistent.

The pioneers of CCM made a way in the musical wilderness for those who followed them. Today's CCM groups reap the benefits won by their brothers and sisters in Christ who made their records in garages, sold them out of station wagons, lived from free-will offering to free-will offering, and traveled across the country singing at Jesus Festivals. Thanks to them, a group like Petra can perform before 429,000 people on two continents. Thanks to them, the Rez Band plays eighty-five concerts a year and has sold more than half a million records. Thanks to them, contemporary Christians have a musical style that appeals to them and lyrics that minister and uplift.

There are lots of reasons CCM has stayed around when

other pieces of the Jesus Movement didn't. One is the quality of its artists. Many were stars in the secular music scene who found that, though fame and fortune did not satisfy, a life with Christ did. Some of these include Leon Patillo (lead singer of Santana), Joe English (drummer/vocalist with Paul McCartney and Wings), Richie Furay (Buffalo Springfield and Poco), Johnny Rivers, Dan Peek (America), Bernie Leadon (the Eagles), and Mylon LeFevre. Their professionalism and commitment to good music (lyrically and musically) have given CCM a boost it needed.

Other names are unfamiliar except to those who are CCM fans (and they are many). Names like Stryper, Sheila Walsh, Steve Taylor, and Leslie Phillips. But even their good-sounding good news is gaining recognition among regular rockers. Jessy Dixon, a black CCM'er, toured with Paul Simon on his "Rhymin' Simon" concerts. One of CCM's most enduring and endearing groups was the Sweet Comfort Band. During their years together they performed in a number of places on the same bill as Fleetwood Mac and the Beach Boys. Greg Volz, formerly of Petra, was asked to audition for an opening in REO Speedwagon. All of this points to first-rate performers—whatever their record label—who are recognized by their peers in the music industry.

Production has also kept pace. Michael Omartian, producer of Christopher Cross's Grammy-Award-winning album and current producer of Jermaine Jackson, Peter Cetera, and others, is heavily involved in CCM. His success in the secular music world has allowed him to build a studio in his house. This allows him to save money producing quality CCM albums for Christian artists. While Christopher Cross's third album cost around $350,000 to record and Amy Grant's *Unguarded* cost $200,000, a CCM disc *can* be cut for about $80,000. Debby Boone's *Choose Life* was, because Omartian did most of the work in his home-based studio and didn't have to charge regular studio rates.

Some CCM artists work with the best studios and performers. The Muscle Shoals, Alabama, recording studios, long known in the secular world for their great musicians and sound, are booked regularly with CCM artists. Some of Muscle Shoals' musicians have become Christians in the past few years. One of them, Ronnie Eades, has chosen to work exclusively on CCM recording projects, even though he doesn't come close to making what he could on a secular record. Thanks to such involvement by Ronnie and others, the sound quality of many CCM discs rivals anything the big boys (CBS, Atlantic, RCA) put out.

By American business standards, CCM is a success. With performers, production, and marketing that rival those in the secular world, CCM garners a larger share of the retail market every year. It has even gone international, with CCM product being released in Great Britain, Spain, Australia, the Far East, and even the Soviet Union. To be sure, most secular rockers don't have to worry about CCM stealing their fans. Still, most major labels are involved in CCM to some degree, either in production or distribution. They realize that there's a lot of money to be made in CCM.

Chris Christian asked, "Why does the devil have all the good music?" Larry Norman asked, "Why should the devil have all the good music?" and then went about making sure he didn't. CCM has come a long way. The sound rivals secular rock. The shows do, too. Mass marketing has gotten it into K mart. This all is good. But it also raises some questions.

9

Has Success Spoiled CCM?

Contemporary Christian music—one of the fastest growing musical forms. Markets in every major (and some not so major) metropolitan area. Concerts that draw thousands. Records on *Billboard* charts. All of this is really great. Or is it?

Though we often feel uncomfortable scrutinizing anything labeled "Christian," that's no excuse for not checking it out. While seeing something labeled Christian should mean that we can be assured it is the best it possibly can be, that's not always the case. To put religious phrases in front of something doesn't guarantee that it is what it should be. Take a lot of "Christian television" for instance. Much of it has very little to do with the Christianity of the Bible and a lot more to do with the American dream of being wealthy. And that's just one example. We need to look critically at everything, even those who call themselves Christians. We need to ask, Is this really Christian? Does what it says fit with what Jesus said? That includes the musical phenomenon known as CCM. We need to ask if success has spoiled CCM. Is it ministry or entertainment? Is it a prophet or for profit?

In spite of everything that seems to be good about CCM,

there are some who say that rock cannot be "saved." They claim that the depth of the lyrics and the positive Christian emphasis do not matter. Radio and TV evangelist Jimmy Swaggart calls Christian rock "spiritual fornication." This in spite of the fact that the music he plays (and records and sells) sounds very much like the rock of the fifties, which his cousin Jerry Lee Lewis helped start. For more on this see Davin Seay's book *Stairway to Heaven*.

According to Swaggart, and many others, it's the beat that's bad. These opponents of CCM try to build a case saying that it triggers primal physical responses. To some extent they are right. Dr. Richard Mountford, chairman of the Fine Arts Division and professor of music at Malone College, says:

> Today we know more about the way music affects us physically and emotionally. Researchers have documented the physical and emotional effects we all experience in music. They've found that music does, at times, affect us physically and emotionally. Music can produce marked physical changes in heart and respiratory rate, blood pressure, neural response in the skin, dilation of the eyes, and muscle contraction and relaxation. This suggests that music's physical effects can be formidable. We can experience these physical changes, however, at an exciting basketball game or in an erotic encounter.
>
> I use the word can rather than does, because not everyone responds to the same music in the same way, unless the music is associated with ceremonies that everyone understands and has experienced. Important variables determine physical response to a given piece of music—e.g.

the degree to which music is important in our lives; the degree of familiarity with the specific piece of music or the musical style being heard; whether or not we like the music; the abruptness of tempo changes in the music; and our mood at the time.

Take, for example, the "altar call" in our evangelical churches. We use hymns such as "Just As I Am" only at the end of the service. Our responses to these hymns (signals) may range from a release of guilt to unexplained feelings of guilt. We use these hymns at this point in the service because they tend to produce a thoughtful introspective mood in the congregation. We believe that such a mood will cause the nonbeliever to examine himself and to respond positively to the "altar call." While the "altar call" hymn does work on the nonbeliever at times, it also signals believers who have not divorced their faith from their feelings, to produce invalid and seductive feelings of guilt. It's hard for us to resist this, and we should understand the effect it has on us.

Undeniably, we do respond physically and emotionally to music. Specific responses to music, however, depend upon individual tastes, environments and associations. Investigators have even found it difficult to get consistent responses to the same piece of music even within the same individuals, since moods and feelings vary from time to time. So, we can't really predict our response to music.[1]

Mountford's article, from which the above was taken, is titled "Rock Music: Can It Rule the Soul?" As he has shown, rock—Christian or secular—has no more control over us than does any other kind of music, including church music. Swaggart's giving CCM an evil nature based simply on its melodic construction merely displays use of outrageous rhetoric to cover up lack of concrete evidence. Once again it's musical taste, not objective reasons, being held up as a moral standard. It's especially sad that a man who claims to have given his life over to the winning of souls for Christ's kingdom can so easily condemn a medium that is winning people daily, many of whom would never think of coming to one of his campaigns. This does not mean his crusades are worthless. They are not. But his biased curse on CCM because it's not what he likes, even though garbed in religious rhetoric and spiritual statements, is wrong.

While CCM is due some criticism, it's not in the area of beat, no matter what Swaggart and others would want us to believe. It is in the area of lyrics. But it's easy to see why lyrics like the ones we will look at shortly have the ability to minister to the people of God. And coupled with a familiar beat, they can reach those who would never respond to a sermon by a TV preacher, no matter how empassioned. I get the feeling that Swaggart, if he'd been alive, probably wouldn't have approved of Martin Luther coupling beer hall tunes familiar to the German masses with religious lyrics, either. And yet, Luther, by so doing, gave us some of the great songs of the faith—songs like "A Mighty Fortress Is Our God."

CCM has the power to move people in ways secular music never will. It can do that because instead of just raising questions it can point to the Answer.

CCM's commercial success has attracted attention. Secular labels know a good thing when they see it. Formerly dominated by exclusively Christian companies like Word, Myrrh, Sparrow, Maranatha! Music, and Milk and Honey, CCM is now seeing major labels getting involved in big ways. A & M is working closely with Word on the production and distribution of Amy Grant's recordings. Some earlier efforts, such as CBS's Priority label, didn't work out. But the potential for excellent production and the mass market is there. This would benefit everyone—the artists, consumers, and record companies. But most of all it would benefit the gospel—by getting it in front of more people than ever before.

Unfortunately, since major labels are getting involved, the question of marketing the gospel has come up. Secular companies are involved in CCM because of its potential as a profit maker. No matter how altruistic they want us to think they are, this is the only reason. What it means is that sometimes records have been rushed to market to fulfill the consumer's need for product. While thought is given to content (usually controlled by the record company), quality of lyrics is usually the last thing to be considered. The content that matters is how a piece sounds musically. Is its melody easily remembered? Does it "hook" the listener? Does it have "hit" potential?

CCM album jackets now rival anything that secular labels put out. Early Jesus music records were easy to spot. They featured lots of line drawings and fuzzy photographs. But then the jacket was seen as just a cover for the album, not as a marketing device. Now CCM album covers are often flashy and feature dynamic graphics and photos of the artists. Except for the titles of some of the songs or of the album itself, a CCM release is hard to distinguish from its secular counterparts. If someone mixed up the bins at Musicland, a person picking up a current CCM release would probably not notice, at least at first, that he or she was holding a Christian record. Whether that's good or bad depends on how you think something Christian should appear. What do you think?

Along with the question of marketing comes the question of charging money for religious music. There are those who feel that CCM—music dedicated to the Lord—should be available to anyone who wants it, regardless of their ability to pay. The way much CCM is, this is not possible. As long as companies see CCM as a moneymaking product, there will be profit margin behind it. Prices will have to be high enough to cover production costs, artist royalties, marketing, graphics, and so on, the same as for a secular release. There is a minor debate going on in the CCM community about whether groups should charge for concerts and albums. Among those who feel that profit should not be a basis for the distribution of the Lord's music is Melody Green, widow of CCM artist Keith Green. Through Last Day's Ministries, Green's albums are distributed on a "pay what you can afford" basis. This is a novel approach which flies in the face of typical American business procedures that dictate much of the current marketing of CCM. Again, the question is a big one that defies simple answers. Who's right? Who's wrong? It all depends on what people think the purpose of CCM is.

Disregarding questions about the beat, marketing the gospel, and so on, the main thing we need to look at is the lyrics. As the quality of sound reproduction on CCM discs has soared, has lyrical content kept pace? Michael Card, writer of Amy Grant's smash "El Shaddai" and 1983's Gospel Songwriter of the Year, isn't sure it has. Speaking from his perspective as both a songwriter and biblical scholar (undergraduate and graduate degrees in Biblical Studies), Card says that while the music is getting better, the words aren't. He feels that often there is a "hokeyness" about the way Jesus is presented—the presentation being far too shallow. The Jesus of the songs, Card feels, is often not the Jesus of the Bible. The songs are about *feeling* good and are self-serving.

Noel Paul Stookey is also well known in CCM. Though most of the world recognizes him as Paul of the seemingly ever-young group Peter, Paul, and Mary, he is the writer of "The Wedding Song," "Building Block," and several other popular Christian tunes. His work with the Bodyworks band is regularly critically acclaimed. Noel says part of the problem is that "up to this point most Christian music has been more or less the same, which is 'get saved and everything is all right.' And, as most of us know, that's just the first thing in everything being all right."

These are strong statements—from people inside CCM. Yet they aren't unfair. Depth, or lack of it, in lyrics has to be a concern. Lyrics are, after all, what makes CCM Christian. The style of melodic format is similar to secular rock. Far too often there seems to be just a shallow, sugar-coated message. "I was lost, got saved, have no troubles, am waiting for the Rapture, Praise the Lord" is the theme of many of the discs. They are vain repetitions, seemingly ground out merely to meet the market demand.

"To me, if you use the name Jesus lightly—you sing 'Jesus, Jesus, Jesus' . . . and it's just a way to do music, and you want to somehow sanctify it by putting that name in there, that's just as bad as taking His name in vain," says Patty Grambling of Silverwind.

A quick glance at some CCM releases reveals the good feelings and self-serving trends Michael Card fears. On one recent release, six of the ten songs have the words *I* or *me* or *feelings* in their titles. On another, the songs about Christ's return sound more like pleas to be transported from the white, middle-class blues (inflation, joblessness, and so on) than a joyful hymn to that great and glorious day. Such shallowness must be dealt with. The words do indeed determine the worth.

Many people worry about the effects of hidden and backmasked messages on secular records. They fear that listening to such records will subconsciously direct the listeners toward behavior that is inappropriate for Christians.

Since we've seen that we do indeed learn from repetition, repeated listening to anti-Christian lyrics is a valid concern. There also needs to be an awareness, though, that constant listening to the shallow "Just Jesus and me" type of CCM could lead to becoming shallow Christians. If Christians do nothing but listen to such a simplistic message, they'll always be on the milk of faith and never move on to the meat. They'll be followers of the Lord who grow up believing that Christianity is all peaches and cream and none of the hard stuff of life. And that if there is hard stuff in their lives, they must not be living the really spiritual life they've heard about on records.

Card feels that to avoid such a scary scenario, CCM must learn to praise God in profound ways, using Scripture as a foundation. He feels that there is a cleansing going on, that artists involved in CCM for reasons other than ministry are pulling out. Those who remain, he says, must answer the question "Am I on the Lord's side?" He points to Leon Patillo as a CCMer who is involved in it because of ministry. His musical content, says Card, reflects that commitment.

As mentioned earlier, Noel Stookey is an important part of the CCM scene. In the sixties, Peter, Paul, and Mary swept the country with hits as diverse as Bob Dylan's "Blowin' in the Wind," their own "Puff the Magic Dragon" and "I Dig Rock and Roll Music," and John Denver's "Jet Plane." Their involvement in the civil rights movement helped to bring that cause to the consciousness of white middle America. Then they abruptly disbanded. One of the reasons was that Noel had made a commitment to Christ. He realized that this commitment meant setting his family life in order. So he went off the road.

Stookey moved his family to the coast of Maine and there began the delicate task of renewing relationships and cultivating his Christian life. As always he kept writing songs. At first he performed them infrequently, often solo. Now reunited with Peter and Mary for occasional (and usually sold-out) "reunions" with the likes of the Boston Pops, Stookey also tours with his own band, Bodyworks, sharing his new life in Christ. And share he does. His songs are no longer mere message songs, but songs with *the* Message—the Good News. Ever the performer, Stookey concerts are funny, sad, stimulating, and involving. He does everything from stand-up comedy and singing to sound effects (his "Tap-Dancing Mouse" routine even got a hall full of staid, quiet Quakers to smile and tap along—very quietly, of course). Always thoughtful, his lyrics often couch the Christian message in inobtrusive ways. Listeners have to think about what they've just heard. He's no believer in simple answers to hard questions. After each concert he comes out to visit with those who linger on. Just like the Peter, Paul, and Mary concerts of old, people come to share what's on their minds. Noel now has more than just his own questions to share, he has some answers.

Noel's freshness and openness is another thing that sets him and other CCM artists apart from their secular counterparts. He's not whisked away in a limousine at the close of a concert, avoiding all contact with the crowd. Noel says one thing that bothers him about today's rock music is the way that the musicians, the performers, are unreachable. Of a Fleetwood Mac concert he had attended, he says that it was as if the band "had drawn shades over their eyes and no one was allowed in." This aloofness from the audience was disheartening. The people had paid to see a performance and that was all they were allowed to see, because there was no interaction between the players and the people. Of his own concerts he says:

> Before I was a Christian, I performed to
> entertain and be entertained. I derived a lot of

satisfaction out of performing. I still do. But now that satisfaction is similar to that you get from doing a favor or kindness for someone. I feel that I'm of service to the people in my audience. I feel that I am of use to somebody out there, either intellectually or because I'm touching an area that they've thought about. Or maybe I've attacked directly a problem that they have been up against, and they need to know that somebody else has had that same problem and overcome it.

My outlook on life is positive. I want it to be of service as it unfolds.[2]

The desire to live a life of service that relates to and helps people is far different from most secular groups' sole desire to amass vast sums of money. The Christian artist has more to communicate than amazing guitar riffs or drum solos. The Christian, in rock as in life, operates from a mind-set unlike that of the world.

CCM, like secular rock, has a message that is unmistakable. Instead of sex and drugs, though, it's the virtues and responsibility of the Christian life, all being extolled with a Top 40 flavor. For fans who love Jesus—and rock—that's good news.

Noel Stookey says, "There is a great dialogue taking place in the Christian community and I think it's wonderful that it has the format of music to be able to do it." Some of the areas he feels are receiving long-needed CCM attention are social justice and peace issues. Groups like the Rez Band back their music with ministry on the streets of Chicago. The songs reflect the social awareness of the Bible. In "Cats and Dogs" on the album *Film at Eleven* Pat Terry sings:

Well they're blowing up Belfast
The British are bombing the Argentines
And I wonder if we're gonna last
Past this nuclear nightmare scene

raising questions about Christians' attitudes toward war and peace and how they relate to Jesus' statement, "Blessed are the peacemakers." In "American Fast Food," Randy Stonehill wails:

American fast food, what a stupid way to die
American fast food, order me the jumbo fries
Oh, oh it's easy
It's so easy and trouble free
It's quick and disposable, just like me
If I don't stop eating this greasy
American fast food

and makes us think about the stewardship of our bodies and the amount of money we waste on ourselves while most of the world goes hungry.

Steve Taylor, the son of a Baptist minister and the current master of CCM's satirical new wave has said, "I want to communicate the responsibility we have to live out our faith . . ." And communicate he does, telling everyone that he wants to be a clone because that's what some people think it means to be a Christian—that we all have to think, look, and believe exactly alike. He sings that "Cloneliness is next to Godliness." He's not afraid to tackle the hard subjects, like racism and apartheid. Other Christian artists as well are writing these types of provocative songs.

The profound praise, rooted in the Bible, that Michael Card desires for CCM is also coming to the fore. Writers like himself, who are steeped in Scripture, are making a mark. Amy Grant's aforementioned rendition of Card's "El Shaddai" led her *Age to Age* album to outstanding success—both critical and commercial. Such commercial success points to the need that is present in the Christian community for deep praise music in a modern idiom. Michael Kelly Blanchard is another such writer. His "Be Ye Glad" has been recorded by the group Glad and by Noel Stookey and Bodyworks. It urges the listener:

> *Oh, be ye glad, oh, be ye glad*
> *Every debt that you ever had*
> *Has been paid up in full by the grace of the Lord*
> *Be ye glad, be ye glad, be ye glad.*

There's a lot of good music out there in the CCM format. As a help for those who want to try CCM, but don't know one group from another, there is "Sounds Like . . .," a music comparison chart, in the back of this book. It was put together by Paul Baker, probably the foremost authority on CCM. His book *Contemporary Christian Music* is the most-detailed history of CCM around and includes all sorts of super information, like discographies and more. The chart here lists CCM artists, which secular groups they most sound like, and which style they most closely resemble. Paul's chart has appeared in several publications and is also used by him in seminars across the nation.

The CCM fan has another advantage—besides good lyrics—over his neighbor who lives on regular rock. Most CCM discs can be previewed prior to purchase. Local Christian bookstores are still the biggest outlets for CCM. Many, if not most, of them have demonstration copies of the latest CCM releases that they'll make available to prospective customers. Some even have listening stations, complete with headphones. That way you know what you're buying and always go home a winner. Try asking your local RecordLand to let you preview Springsteen's newest. Guess what happens?

Yet one more advantage is in the area of live concerts. When Billy Joel shows up in your town (if he ever does) expect to pay $17.50 or more for a seat. It'll probably be behind a post. And you'll share the space with some sixteen thousand other concertgoers. Some of whom aren't very nice. They can be rude, crude, and otherwise obnoxious. CCM concerts, on the other hand, tend to be in smaller halls (better acoustics and you're closer to the performers), the crowds are more polite, and the tickets are cheaper. When Joe English came to our town (not Indianapolis, but tiny Plainfield!) he and his band put on a dynamite concert. The auditorium, which only holds a thousand, was full. The band rocked. Really rocked. The crowd went home enthusiastic and ministered to. And it only cost five dollars. A better bargain in music can't be found.

So where does that leave us? Has success spoiled CCM? Yes—and no. In many ways CCM stands at a fork in the road. It can go one way and keep on becoming another American success story—reaping big bucks all the way. Or it can be a servant of the Lord. While these two may not be mutually exclusive, it is clear that the world needs more than another form of mere music—even music with sanitized lyrics. It needs ministry, with sanctified lyrics. The world is hungry for a word from the Lord.

Music is a gift. There is something about it that speaks to our condition. The music that has stood the test of time is most often that which was dedicated to God. To equate Benny Hester and Bach is stretching it a bit. Okay, a whole lot. But there is something special about CCM that gives it stability in a world that is falling apart. That specialness is the message. It is timeless. The Good News never grows old and is needed more today than ever before. If you want really good music, then—listen to the rock that doesn't roll.

---

1. Robert D. Mountford, "Rock Music: Can It Rule the Soul," *The Malone Messenger* (Summer 1983), pp. 9–11. This article was adapted from Dr. Mountford's "Does the Music Make Them Do It?" © 1979 *Christianity Today* (May 4, 1970), and is used by permission. Dr. Mountford also had me in his Music Appreciation class my freshman year. I'm sure he's still recovering from that experience.

2. *Salt Company Newsletter* (South Bend, 1979), p. 5.

10

The Rock of Our Salvation

Jesus Christ, Jesus Christ,
Who are you?
What have you sacrificed?

These are questions that need answers. With this refrain the Rock Generation cries out for answers, using the rock opera *Jesus Christ, Superstar* as its voice.

When *Jesus Christ, Superstar* first burst on the scene, the reactions were varied and extreme. "A work of art," some exclaimed. "Trash and sacrilege," cried others. But to a world soaked in war, LSD, and free love of the early seventies it brought a new view of Jesus. And this new view stimulated interest. Some people looked only through the eyes of Weber and Rice, the composers, and accepted their sympathetic, but skeptical view of Jesus. "He's a man, he's just a man." Others, taking a cue from the Bible verse at the end of the libretto, searched the Scriptures. The questions *Jesus Christ, Superstar* raised were not new ones. They had just been phrased in new ways. They were ways that touched chords in the lives of listeners.

Jesus Christ, who are You? What have You sacrificed? Questions that may seem a bit out of place in a book for Christians about rock. After all, we know the answers. Many of us have heard the gospel since we were wee little. Every December we silently mouth the so-familiar words of the Christmas story as the minister reads them from the Bible. The same old manger is trotted out to be surrounded by a fresh crop of suburban first graders in Dad's cut-down bathrobe, trying to look like Jewish shepherds and wise men. The story of the Babe who came to earth from Heaven may be Good News—but it's old news.

So is the rest of His life. The miracles are no longer mysterious. We are apathetic about the apostles. The Resurrection may raise us from our beds for a sunrise service, but doesn't inspire or awe us enough to keep us awake that Sunday afternoon after dinner. It's not that we don't believe. We do. It's just that it's all so familiar. Sometimes we feel, though hesitant to admit it, *So what? What's it all got to do with me now? What does Jesus have to do with rock and my listening to it?* These are questions only you can answer. No one else can—or even has the right to. Not your parents, pastor, or best friend. You are the only one who can decide. And decide you must. Just as Jesus asked Peter, He asks you, "Who do you say that I am?"

Before you rattle off your memorized, completely acceptable answer, think again. How does your heart, as well as your head, answer? Since we have heard it all before, we think we know it all. It may be that we need to hear it again. This time a little differently. So in the tradition of the Master Storyteller, we present a modern-day parable.

Now the kingdom of God is like a gas station. Back when God decided to begin making automobiles, He set up the universe's only service station. Since it was the only one, and God had made all the cars in the first place, it was the natural place to go. The work was inexpensive—all God required, was allegiance and love—and guaranteed.

Then came competition—in the guise of Sam Satan. God wasn't too worried. After all He had made it all, including Sam. It was He who had given Sam his start. Taught him everything he knew. But Sam had ideas of his own. He wasn't content working with God and he wanted out. So he left.

God's Good Gas was a rather nondescript place on an out-of-the-way straight, but narrow, road. It was built for the business of keeping cars running right and was not at all showy. It attracted hardly any attention. Besides, the humans were in too much of a hurry to use this narrow, little-traveled road. So they built superhighways, eight lanes in each direction, to help get them to the places they were in such a frantic fit to get to. To get gas at God's, they had to exit the freeway, slow down, and drive more sedately than they cared to.

Sam, being shrewd (but not all that competent when it came to cars), decided that location was the name of the game. So he had *his* station built right in the middle of the sixteen lanes of the biggest freeway around. He installed wide exits and entrance ramps leading from the freeway to his station to the freeway again. The building itself was made of the most gleaming white porcelained steel that ever graced a service station. Thousands of brightly colored festive flags festooned the entrance, whipping in the wind. Row upon row of gasoline pumps stood like toy soldiers at attention atop a child's chest of drawers. And there were giveaways, too. None of the NFL matchbook sets or TV trays covered in genuine simulated leather-look vinyl, either. No, sir. Sam's folks offered your heart's desire. And to top it all, there was the sign. Towering a hundred feet in the air, it was a marvel. Perched on top were the proud words *Satan's Place*. The Great Gas Giveaway wars had begun.

Very few folks realized how bad Satan's Place was. All they saw was that it was easy to get to, looked nice, and offered great prizes. Beneath the shiny surface the place was a farce. Built hurriedly out of second-rate and worse materials, the exterior was only a covering that hid a lack of substance in the building. Sam himself was only a caricature of a car mechanic. He hadn't been with God long enough to really learn anything. But he thought he knew it all. That is why he wanted to be on his own. He was tired of being the hired hand. He'd show God.

As little as Sam knew, his workers knew even less. They didn't know a screwdriver from the horns on their heads. The gas in the pumps was watered down, the oil they used had already been used in another car, and the rest rooms were really filthy. There was never any work done on a car, though the customer was told there was. Which meant that they had to come back more and more often to get the car fixed. Which it never was.

Sam relied on his location and his charm to get people to come in. And his credit system. "Buy now, pay later" was the motto. No matter that God's original warranty was for the life of the car, which made service almost free. But Satan had the giveaways. "A little sex, some booze or drugs? Name what you want, cousin. Here, take and enjoy." So people took, got in their cars, and rambled on down the road. The car still didn't run right, but who cared? Let's bring it in tomorrow and have it worked on again—and get some more goodies.

Sam Satan came across as a good old boy. God didn't extend credit to the humans, now did He? Everyone soon forgot about God's place. No one really noticed (probably because it was written in invisible ink) Sam's 1000 percent interest—compounded hourly.

Soon, due to lack of service, the cars would break down. Satan's helpers then came to collect. Since no one had the kind of money Sammy's bill came to, they'd just take the owner's soul instead. After all, the fine print, but not in invisible ink for a change, said they could. So they did. This happened all the time. But the others tried not to notice. Don't want to miss the giveaways you know.

Meanwhile, God's place kept working on the few cars that did keep coming in. His factory-trained mechanics made sure that each auto continued to run like new. The owners were happy and automobile ownership was like it was meant to be.

But God was sad. He was happy for those smart enough to still stop by, but His heart was breaking for those who went to Satan's Place. Tears rolled down His cheeks when He saw yet another of His once-shiny creations now rusted and ruined being hauled off to the junkyard, its owner bankrupt. He had to do something. Then the idea came. The greatest giveaway of them all. A graceful warranty.

God decided that while people knew the rules about keeping their cars running right, many of them somehow just couldn't seem to follow them. So He decided to give them another chance. Whichever of the humans brought their autos into God's place would find their debts to Satan canceled and their cars set to running right—forever. All they had to do was come in, say they were sorry for the auto abuse, and begin God's service again.

What God needed was a way to get the word out to the people.

God sent John D. Baptist out to the freeway. He stood in the middle of Sam Satan's Place and hollered out what God had told him to say. "Make ready the Lord's road, for the Great Giveaway is a coming." Now, John was a sort of backwoods mechanic God had trained, not very tactful or long on grammar, but he got people's attention. They stopped what they were doing, got out of their cars, and came over to listen. His announcement had them all abuzz.

Finally John said, "That Great Giveaway I've been a tellin' you about? Well, here it is."

And out stepped Jesus.

And Jesus said, "Here I am, take Me. As the only Son of the Manufacturer and a Master Mechanic myself, I'll make your old cars like new. I'll make them run and run abundantly. I'll fix them so that they'll run *forever*. All you have to do is accept My Daddy's offer."

The crowd went wild. Just think, to never have a car problem again. Then Jesus spoke again. This time a little more quietly, but just as forcefully.

"But you've got to promise to let Me be your *only* mechanic."

The crowd fell quiet. People shuffled their feet. Then one by one the sound of starters shattered the silence. Tires crunched the gravel berm and shushed down the highway. Only a few remained. These were hard sayings.

This time God didn't cry alone. Jesus shared His tears.

Those who dared to stay behind found that life seemed a lot more meaningful. Though the change in the car from the first tune-up was radical, it was only a beginning. Every day the car seemed to run stronger and smoother. The drives on God's road, though not as fast, were exciting. Since the landscape was no longer merely a sideline blur on the way from one smog-filled metropolis to another, the beauty of creation came to be enjoyed. The drivers found they liked clear air, cool water, birds singing, and long talks with God and other travelers. Life got sweeter as the miles went by.

God's place isn't hard to find. It's aways off from most of the traffic. It's still open, too. And the Great Giveaway still goes on. Need a tune-up?

Stories can be fun. They often contain truth, as well. I hope this one had both—fun and truth. It is of course a shadow of the whole Truth. One cannot write the gospel in three or four pages. But the truth is—mysterious as it seems—God loves us, wants the best for us, and has offered His grace to us. That's a miracle.

God gave His Son because He loves us tiny humans. Jesus gave Himself so that we might be able to live life as fully as it was meant to be lived. That living is for now.

We may look at Jesus and say that He demands too much. The life He expects us to live is too hard. And not much fun. Look at all we'll have to give up. Yet, what does He ask, other than to be allowed into our lives in order to set them right and make them complete? That means we have to admit we have made mistakes and done things that haven't been on the up-and-up. But our own insides tell us that. There's something deep inside us that tells us we are not as we should be. Jesus simply asks that we confess that we are not the final authority, that we haven't always done what was right, and that we need His help in our lives.

Jesus does have something to do with rock, because it's a part of our lives. And Jesus is interested in each part of our lives. Since He wants the best for us, and rock isn't always the best, He may say some things to you on that subject. But be assured, nothing can separate us from the love of God— not even rock and roll.

"Jesus Christ, Jesus Christ. Who are You, what have You sacrificed?" Jesus said. "I am the Way, the Truth, and the Life." And He sacrificed Himself—for you and me. What more could He do?

Rock is a thrill. Every day some sort of rock is either introduced or reintroduced. Techno-rock, new wave, rockabilly, punk, acid, on and on. The rock thrills keep coming. And wearing off. But there is something that continues to thrill and never gets dull. If we want it, we need to hang on to the Solid Rock.

Strata

Webster's defines *strata* as "layers of rock." Below you will find musical strata—alphabetized rock. Just as layers of rock in our planet often seem to melt into one another, with no clear-cut dividing line, the same is true of types of musical rock. While the categories listed below are meant to be helpful, they are by no means rigid. A song that is considered adult contemporary could also be classified dance or black. This is because rock is commercial, and its producers wish to reach as many listeners as possible. Therefore they try to "cross over" these distinctions.

The strata listed below are not all-inclusive. True musical geologists will pick out glaring omissions. The list is meant for the layperson, one who wants to know the major types of rock at a glance. As a quick reference tool, I think you'll find it handy.

Acid Rock—is identified with the San Francisco scene of the late sixties and early seventies. Use of Indian raga styles, with sitars and other instruments not normally connected with pop music, was the norm. The lyrical content was usually of little substance, with a great deal of emphasis on drugs and free love. There was often some anti-Vietnam-War sentiment thrown in for good measure. The acid in acid rock came from street slang for LSD. Most notable players: Jefferson Airplane, the Doors, Janis Joplin, and Jimi Hendrix.

Adult Contemporary—is rock geared for those over twenty-five. It tends to focus on clarity of vocals and nice harmonies rather than making your ears bleed. It is an over-all soft sound, but doesn't sacrifice the back beat. Adult contemporary embraces a wide range of styles from country-western to new wave to black—provided the songs are more mellow than usual. Adult contemporary also includes the playing of golden oldies. Most notable players: Lionel Richie, Neil Diamond, Dan Fogelberg, and Carly Simon.

Black—is what used to be called soul music. It leans more to the pure rhythm and blues than does most of rock. Black music is aimed at young, black, urban audiences in the large metropolitan areas. It has a long and impressive history, and many of its stars have been around quite a while. Heavy into stylization and beat, black music always seems to be influencing mainstream rock. Most notable players: Aretha Franklin, Billy Ocean, Anita Baker, and Freddie Jackson.

Bubblegum—is largely what its name implies—sickeningly sweet with not much substance. Invented as a way to garner the greenies of the teenybopper set (those fourteen and under), it had its largest popularity in the mid- to late-sixties. Most of the groups were made up of studio musicians for the purpose of recording bubblegum. One group, the Archies, was in reality a cartoon series. Bubblegum was in many respects the ultimate commercialization of rock, created to make a new market. Though not as popular now as it once was, it continues to surface occasionally. Most notable players: 1910 Fruitgum Company, David Cassidy, the Ohio Express, and Shaun Cassidy.

Country Rock—is a mellow, laid-back type of rock. It makes use of C & W style harmonies and instrumentals. The usual rock instruments are augmented with slide guitars, dobros, fiddles, and the like. Linda Ronstadt is often considered the first lady of country rock because of her music of the mid-seventies. Juice Newton seems to be her heir apparent, as Ronstadt has changed her style to a more pop-oriented one. Most notable players: the Eagles, Alabama, and Eddie Rabbitt.

Disco—grew out of the gay bars on the East Coast. As it spread, it began to appeal to a heterosexual, urban, southeastern crowd and picked up the Miami sound, epitomized by K.C. and the Sunshine Band. The movie *Saturday Night Fever* propelled disco into the national consciousness. With great emphasis on production, lots of strings, horns, all put together with an electric rhythm, disco swept the nation. Many rockers made disco hits, many others rejected the sound as meaningless. It soon began to wane, and is once again mostly on the coasts. Disco is now mostly known as dance music, and its stars are usually not that well-known by most rock listeners. Most notable players: the Bee Gees, Donna Summer, and Yaz.

Folk Rock—is a natural blending of California pop rock (i.e., the Beach Boys) and the folk movement. It usually came out sounding like folk music with a back beat. The first truly popular folk rock song was "Sounds of Silence" by Simon and Garfunkel, which had failed miserably as an acoustic release. Folk rock featured lots of acoustic guitars and tight harmonies. Still popular today, it most often is classified adult contemporary. Most notable players: Crosby, Stills, Nash, and Young; Simon and Garfunkel; the Byrds; and Bob Dylan.

Glitter Rock—was the harbinger of punk and new wave. Bored with the rock of the mid-seventies, glitter came along with its reliance on makeup, theatrics, and costumes that were zany even by rock standards. The music was loud and stage antics meant to startle the audience. It coupled the sheer volume of hard rock with flashpots, fireworks, and other visuals. Most notable players: T. Rex, David Bowie (as Ziggy Stardust), and KISS.

Hard Rock—puts its emphasis on an almost inpenetrable wall of sound. Rock has always utilized the back beat—bass and drums pounding away—but hard rock takes it one step further. By using the most powerful amplifiers around, hard rock puts out a back beat that is felt as much as it is heard. Hard rock musicians are known to wear earplugs at times to prevent hearing loss from the sheer volume of sound. Most notable players: Foreigner, Allman Brothers, and Golden Earring.

Heavy Metal—is a lot harder than hard rock. Heavy metal groups often rely on theatrics, showmanship, light shows, flashpots, and the like. Outrageous costumes, bizarre album covers, and often indecipherable lyrics (which is usually just as well) complete the ensemble. Most notable players: Judas Priest, Van Halen, and Twisted Sister.

New Wave—is the cleaned-up offspring of punk rock. New wave is largely a rebellion against the rock superstar system of the late 1970s. It tends to stand against whatever its artists consider bland, boring, or taken too seriously. The music is generally offbeat, played with a sense of humor. There is novelty both of dress and musical style. Anything goes in new wave—as long as it isn't pretentious or self-important. New wave is a return to basic rock, with a driving beat, fast music, and straight-out melodies. Most notable players: Devo, Joe Jackson, and Talking Heads.

Pop Rock—is smoothly executed, middle-of-the-road rock. Popular mostly in the mid-sixties, it was made up of two- to three-minute songs with decent lyrics and good beat—and it was easy to dance to. Never on the cutting edge of musical or lyrical content, it is safe for AM radio and small children. Most pop rock today is classified adult contemporary. Most notable players: the Association, the Turtles, Pablo Cruise, the Carpenters, and ABBA.

Punk—was the follower of glitter rock and forebear of new wave. Ostensibly a return to the roots of rock, with its short-format songs and driving beat, it is often contrived to shock. Punk adherents wore safety pins in their cheeks and did other such obnoxious things. The lyrics are often nihilistic in nature, as the world is seen to be worthless. Punk as a popular style never caught on until it cleaned up and metamorphosed into new wave. Most notable players: the Ramones, Iggy Pop, and Billy Idol.

Rockabilly—is the earliest form of rock, now enjoying a great resurgence. Rockabilly leans toward the country side of rock the way black leans toward the R & B. Most early rock was rockabilly, so called because it was a cross between rock and "hillbilly" music. Early rockabilly stars include Buddy Holly and the Crickets and Jerry Lee Lewis. A rockabilly revival is currently under way in rock circles. Most notable players: Elvis Presley, the Stray Cats, any early rock and roller.

Soft Rock—see adult contemporary.

Techno-pop—is a form of new wave that relies heavily on synthesizers and other audio effects. This is no simple guitars and drums stuff. Very eclectic in style, some of the best-known techno-pop songs have been reworkings of older songs. Taco's "Puttin' On the Ritz" is an example. Most notable players: Human League, the Eurythmics, and Emerson, Lake, and Powell.

Old Time Rock and Roll—is everything else not listed here. While not made up of "Golden Oldies," it's certainly inspired by them. This covers everything from Bruce Hornsby and the Range's "The Way It Is" to Bruce Springsteen's "Born in the USA." Most notable players: Bruce Springsteen, Huey Lewis and the News, Bob Seger and the Silver Bullet Band.

Rock Themes A to Z

T. Canby Jones, professor of religion and philosophy at Wilmington College in Ohio, says that rock and roll is "four notes and four words repeated for four minutes." Many people agree with him. Rock is often perceived as mindless lyrics revolving around the same old subjects. That is far from true. Rock, since its earliest days, has always been concerned with anything and everything that people think about. The topics range from the sublime to the ridiculous. The list below, while far from being all-inclusive, should give you an idea just how wide-ranging rock themes are.

A   Automobiles—"Hot Rod Lincoln," by Johnny Bond, covered by Commander Cody and His Lost Planet Airmen.

B   Bananas—"30,000 Pounds of Bananas," by Harry Chapin.

C   Christmas—"Rockin' Around the Christmas Tree," by Brenda Lee.

D   Dogs—"Hound Dog," by Elvis Presley.

E   Equal Rights—"Blowin' in the Wind," by Bob Dylan, covered by Peter, Paul, and Mary.

F   Flying—"Jet Airliner," by the Steve Miller Band.

G   Gorillas—"Harry, the Hairy Ape," by Ray Stevens.

H   Hotels—"Hotel California," by the Eagles.

I   Imagination—"Just My Imagination (Running Away With Me)," by the Temptations.

J   Jobs—"She Works Hard for the Money," by Donna Summer.

K   Kansas City—"Kansas City," by Wilbert Harrison.

L   Love—"Lost in Love," by Air Supply.

M   Monsters—"Monster Mash," by Bobby "Boris" Pickett.

N   Nighttime—"In the Still of the Nite," by the Five Satins.

O   Onions—"Green Onions," by Booker T. and the MGs.

P   Psychiatry—"Nervous Breakdown," by Eddie Cochran.

Q   Queens—"Queen of the Broken Hearts," by Loverboy.

R   Roofs—"Up on the Roof," by the Drifters, covered by James Taylor.

S   Sun—"Here Comes the Sun," by the Beatles.

T   Tears—"Tracks of My Tears," by Smokey Robinson.

U   Uptown—"Uptown," by the Crystals.

V   Vanity—"You're So Vain," by Carly Simon.

W   Walking—"Walk Like a Man," by the Four Seasons.

X   Xenophobia—"There's a Stranger in My House," by Ronny Milsap.

Y   Yellow—"Mellow Yellow," by Donovan.

Z   Zoos—"At the Zoo," by Simon and Garfunkel.

Questions and Discussion Starters

Use the following questions and suggestions to help begin discussion on the sensitive subject of rock. They can be utilized by parents and teens individually or in a family setting. Be open and honest in your responses. There are no right or wrong answers. Simply use them as a tool to help determine your feelings about rock and roll.

1. Write your definition of rock and roll, using twenty-five words or less. Using the following scale, rate your opinion of rock

   1--10
   Devil's Dirt Pile   Simply Super Stuff

   Why did you put it where you did?

   Of the following types of music, is one any worse than another? Rate them with 1 being the best and 8 the worst.
   —Classical
   —Country and western
   —Folk
   —Hard rock

—Jazz
—Light classics
—Pop rock
—Rhythm and blues

What makes one form better or worse than another?

2. Do your own evaluation of rock by comparing an early rock and roll song with a current hit. Check them for musical style and lyrical content. Are there any differences? Are there meanings that seem hidden in one that are out in the open in the other? Which is worse, hidden or overt? Why?

3. Do you think sex, drugs, and cheap thrills make up too large a portion of rock themes? How should Christians respond to songs of questionable moral content? Outline a course of action below.

    I. Define the problem (what's wrong with the song)

A.

B.

    II. Christian response

A.

B.

4. Get recordings or lyric sheets of the current Top 5. Why do you think these songs are so popular? Circle your response(s).

    Well-known recording star
    Easy to dance to
    Topic rockers are interested in
    Excellent instrumentals
    Good beat
    Super lyrics
    Unusual sound
    Popular group

Are these songs positive or negative in the way they treat the subject matter? How do you think Jesus would respond to these songs? Be specific.

5. In your opinion, are rock stars' lives any worse than anybody else's? On what information do you base your opinion? Should you support a person's product when his life-style is contrary to Christianity? Rate the following occupations in regard to their immorality or morality.

Airline Pilots
Doctors
Farmers
Lawyers
Ministers
Nurses
Rock stars
Teachers
Truck drivers
Wrestlers (professional)

Read what Jesus said in Matthew 7:1. After reading that, do we have any right to judge others? Can you find something in the Bible to support your stand?

6. Read Ephesians 5:15–20. Now listen to your favorite rock song. Why do you like it? Does it accurately reflect *your* feelings concerning its subject matter? Do you like what it says? How does it stack up in light of the passage from Ephesians?

7. For Parents: Dig out some of your favorite songs from your teen years. Try to recall what made them meaningful to you. Share them with your kids. Relate some of the good—and bad—experiences you had as a teenager. Try to share things that parallel experiences your youngsters are living. Talk about the relationships you had with your parents, your first true love, your first car, etc. Share how you feel about your teen years as you view them from a parent's eyes. You might want to play Dan Fogelberg's "Leader of the Band" or Jackson Browne's "Daddy's Tune" as a way to get started.

8. How do you feel about Contemporary Christian music? Can rock and roll be Christian? Why or why not? Can a musician who's a Christian play rock that's not? Are there themes that CCM should avoid? Why? What makes music Christian?

9. Do you think Jesus would listen to rock and roll? What do you feel His attitude would be toward it? Is there ONE Christian position? Pick the listener below who is closest to where you are now.

    1. Cathy Christian—she only listens to CCM. She likes rock, but doesn't want to have to worry about the words.

    2. Suzi Selective——she likes rock and roll, but worries about some of its messages. She is careful about what she buys and listens to.

    3. Roger Rockenroll—he listens to everything the radio plays. If it is on "American Top 40," it's got to be good.

    4. Bobby Burnemup—he feels that any and all rock is bad. No Christian should listen to the stuff. Plays other types of music.

Why do you feel that your position is the best? Is one any better than the rest? Do you feel comfortable with your present position—or should you consider a change?

Rockin' Resources

There are lots of good resources out there if you want to learn more about rock and roll. Listed below are just some of what's available.

Baker, Paul. *Contemporary Christian Music.* Crossway Books, 1985. Originally published in 1979 as *Why Should the Devil Have All the Good Music,* this is the most comprehensive commentary available on CCM. Though it first appeared in 1979, Baker has completely updated it so that it covers most everything about CCM a person would want to know. In addition to the text it includes "The Contemporary Christian Music Family Tree—1963-1978" and " 'Religious' Songs Which Reached the *Billboard* Top 100 Pop Charts 1955-1984." This is an excellent book for anyone who wants a behind-the-scenes look at CCM.

Hancock, Jim. *The Rock and Roll Teacher.* Youth Specialties, 1986. This is a Christian education curriculum that uses rock and roll as a teaching tool. There are ten lessons on all sorts of current topics. A stereo cassette comes with the course and features ten songs by some of CCM's top recording artists.

The Parent's Music Resource Center. Not a book, or a curriculum, the PMRC is a resource center developed by concerned parents. They have done exhaustive studies on rock and roll and how it affects us. Their studies of lyrics will tell you everything you want to know—and a lot you don't—about the state of today's music. Especially enlightening are their exposés of "heavy metal." They have also produced "Rise to the Challenge"—a twenty-minute VHS cassette that takes a look at today's popular music. It is for adults only. "Let's Talk Rock: A Parent's Primer" is their handbook of advice. "Rock Music Report" is a thirty-minute audiocassette that includes current music, quotes from music industry folks and musicians. All of these, and more, are available from the PMRC, 1500 Arlington Blvd., Arlington, VA 22209.

Rabey, Steve. *The Heart of Rock and Roll.* Fleming H. Revell, 1986. Rabey takes the reader on a pictorial tour of the lives and ministries of ten of CCM's best-known artists. Filled with full-color pictures, lots of lyrics for illustration, and readable text, *The Heart of Rock and Roll* gives good insight into the personalities of the ten lives highlighted.

Romanowksi, Patricia, and Pareles, Jon. *The Rolling Stone Encyclopedia of Rock & Roll.* Summit Books, 1983. This is probably the most comprehensive one-volume work around on the real stuff of rock and roll. If you believe everything you read about rock stars in *People* or the *National Enquirer,* you'll find the encyclopedia rather tame. You will learn about every group, artist, and type of music that was around when the book was published.

Seay, Davin, and Neely, Mary. *Stairway to Heaven: The Spiritual Roots of Rock and Roll,* Ballantine Epiphany, 1986. This book takes a behind-the-scenes look at the spiritual struggles of some of rock and roll's biggest stars. The authors show how religion has had an effect on rock and roll, its lyrics, performers, and their life-styles. Interesting comparisons are made of two famous cousins—singer Jerry Lee Lewis and evangelist Jimmy Swaggart. A must read.

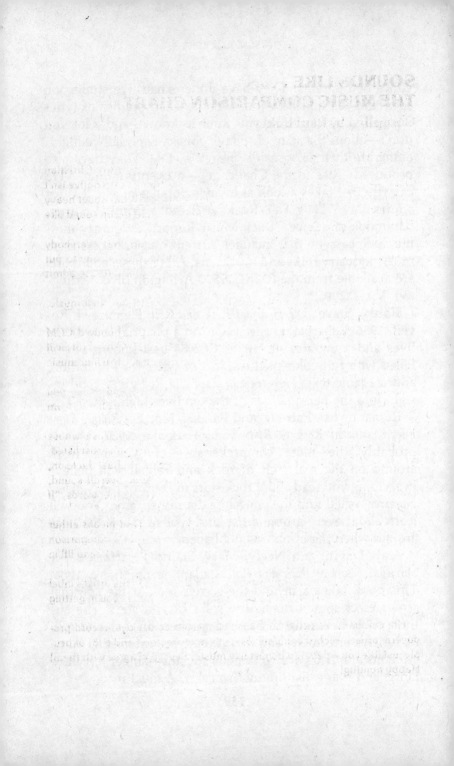

SOUNDS LIKE . . .
THE MUSIC COMPARISON CHART
Compiled by Paul Baker

What's your favorite style of music?

No matter what it is, there's probably some contemporary Christian music that will fit your tastes. But finding that Christian alternative isn't always so easy. Who does new wave? Who's into folk? What about heavy metal? Do any Christians do jazz? Does any Christian group sound like ABBA? And who sounds like Huey Lewis and the News?

Be thou not dismayed. Help is here! It's the chart that everybody wanted, but only a few had the courage, patience, and tenacity to put together. The list everyone was curious about, but no one dared to admit it!

It's the Grand Tour of contemporary Christian musicians, their music, and what their music sounds like.

On the following pages, we've listed more than two hundred CCM artists and a *general* description of their musical styles. Perhaps this will help you get started in finding a form of contemporary Christian music that suits your tastes, or a friend's.

Of course, the list is only for getting your bearings and giving you general ideas. It's very arbitrary, because artists' styles may change from time to time, from record to record, and even from song to song.

The comparisons here show one or more pop recording artists whose music is performed in the same general style as the Christian artist listed. But just because the chart says an artist resembles Michael Jackson, doesn't mean that artist can sing high C. It compares *overall* sound, performing style, and genre, or even songwriting style. In other words, "If you like so-and-so, there's a good chance you'll like so-and-so."

In some cases, the "sounds like" column is blank. That means either that the artist has his or her own unique sound, or that a comparison hadn't been determined when this chart was prepared. Feel free to fill in the blanks yourself!

If you see a record that might interest you, the name of the artist's label is provided right next to the Christian artist's name to help you in getting albums by that artist.

The comparisons listed here were suggested by deejays, record producers, artists, record company executives, collectors, and a lot of people just like you—people who just like music. See if you agree with them! Happy hunting!

Sounds Like...

ARTIST & LABEL	RESEMBLES	CLUB ROCK/DANCE	TECHNO-POP/SYNTH-ROCK	NEW MUSIC/NEW WAVE	HEAVY METAL	HARD ROCK	ROCK	POP ROCK/ADULT CONTEMPORARY	ROCKABILLY/NOSTALGIC ROCK	SOUTHERN ROCK	HEARTLAND ROCK	CLASSICAL ROCK/ORCHESTRAL ROCK	JAZZ/JAZZ FUSION	ISLAND/LATIN/AFRICAN	RAP	SOUL BALLAD	BLUES	SOUL/RHYTHM & BLUES/FUNK	BLACK GOSPEL	COUNTRY ROCK	COUNTRY	FOLK/FOLK ROCK	ACOUSTIC	BALLAD	CLASSICAL	PRAISE/HYMNS/TRADITIONAL SACRED	POP/MIDDLE-OF-THE-ROAD	BIG BAND/SWING	INSTRUMENTAL	CONTEMPLATIVE/MEDITATIVE/MOOD
A.D. (Kerygma)	Kansas; Toto; Foreigner; Journey; Survivor; REO Speedwagon		★				★	★				★												★						
Simon Adahl (Refuge)	Phil Collins; Eurythmics; Robert Plant		★					★																						
Adam Again (Blue Collar)	A-ha; Prince; Wham; ABC; Donna Allen; Talking Heads		★	★											★			★												
Dennis Agajanian (Sparrow)	Eddie Rabbitt; Gordon Lightfoot; Johnny Lee								★											★	★	★	★							
Allies (Light)	Journey; Kansas; Survivor; Boston; Steve Perry; Foreigner; Glass Tiger						★	★																★						
Justo Almario (Meadowlark)	(Sax)												★										★	★	★				★	★
Altar Boys (Frontline)	Ramones; Dead Kennedys; Meat Puppets; Night Ranger			★			★																							
Steve Archer (Home Sweet Home)		★	★					★																						
Bob Ayala (Myrrh, Pretty Good)	Harry Chapin																							★			★			
Philip Bailey (Myrrh)	Earth, Wind & Fire; Al Jarreau	★														★		★	★								★			
Tammy Sue Bakker (Eklectic)	Teena Marie; The Bangles; Heart; Madonna							★																★						

Artist	Comparison
Barnabas (Light)	Grace Slick; Joan Jett & the Blackhearts; Queen's Ryche
David Baroni (Lifestream)	
Barren Cross (Star Song, Enigma)	Iron Maiden; Judas Priest; Sammy Hagar; Cinderella
Bash-n-the-Code (Myrrh)	Berlin; Thompson Twins; Duran Duran
Margaret Becker (Sparrow)	Nancy Wilson (of Heart)
Bob Bennett (Star Song)	Bruce Cockburn; James Taylor
Bloodgood (Frontline)	Iron Maiden; Megadeath
Blue Trapeze (Fullspeak, Refuge)	R.E.M.; 10,000 Maniacs
Bodyworks (NewPax)	Rita Coolidge; Jim Croce; Noel Stookey
Debby Boone (Lamb & Lion)	
Kim Boyce (Myrrh)	Madonna; Stacey Q: The Jets
Bride (Pure Metal)	Bon Jovi; Stryper
Scott Wesley Brown (Sparrow)	
Harry Robert Browning (Lamb & Lion)	Rick Springfield
Larry Bryant (Light)	
Shirley Caesar (Myrrh, Rejoice)	
The Call (Elektra)	
Steve Camp (Myrrh, Sparrow)	Paul Young; Jackson Browne; Kenny Loggins
Michael Card (Sparrow)	Dan Fogelberg
Carman (Priority, Myrrh, Benson)	Elvis Presley; Sylvester Stallone
Morris Chapman (Dayspring)	Lou Rawls
Steve & Annie Chapman (Star Song)	Bobby Goldsboro; Anne Murray
Steven Curtis Chapman (Sparrow)	Huey Lewis & the News

Sounds Like...

ARTIST & LABEL	RESEMBLES	CLUB ROCK/DANCE	TECHNO-POP/SYNTH-ROCK	NEW MUSIC/NEW WAVE	HEAVY METAL	HARD ROCK	ROCK	POP ROCK/ADULT CONTEMPORARY	ROCKABILLY/NOSTALGIC ROCK	SOUTHERN ROCK	HEARTLAND ROCK	CLASSICAL ROCK/ORCHESTRAL ROCK	JAZZ/JAZZ FUSION	ISLAND/LATIN/AFRICAN	RAP	SOUL BALLAD	BLUES	SOUL/RHYTHM & BLUES/FUNK	BLACK GOSPEL	COUNTRY ROCK	COUNTRY	FOLK/FOLK ROCK	ACOUSTIC	BALLAD	CLASSICAL	PRAISE/HYMNS/TRADITIONAL SACRED	POP/MIDDLE-OF-THE-ROAD	BIG BAND/SWING	INSTRUMENTAL	CONTEMPLATIVE/MEDITATIVE/MOOD
The Choir (Myrrh)	U2; R.E.M.; Flock of Seagulls; A-ha; Echo & the Bunnymen			★				★																★						
Chris Christian (Myrrh, Home Sweet Home)	Paul Davis							★																★						
Terry Clark (First Fruits)	David Clayton-Thomas																★	★	★					★		★				
Clark Sisters (Rejoice)																			★							★				
Cynthia Clawson (Dayspring)	Barbra Streisand							★																★	★	★	★			
Common Bond (Frontline)	Geddy Lee; INXS; Human League			★			★																							
Copious (Fortress)						★	★																							
Billy Crockett (Dayspring)	Culture Club; Michael Jackson; Crowded House							★					★											★						
Andrae Crouch (Light, Warner Bros.)																★		★	★								★		★	
Robin Crow (Fortress)	Rick Wakeman; Mike Oldfield; ELP; Yes; Al Stewart; Pink Floyd; Larry Carlton; Bruce Cockburn		★				★	★			★	★											★	★		★	★		★	★
Crumbacher (Frontline)	Cars; Human League		★	★																										
Cruse (Greentree)			★					★				★												★			★			

Artist (Label)	Sounds Like
Morgan Cryar (Star Song)	John Waite; Lou Gramm; Don Johnson; Bryan Adams
Rick Cua (Refuge, Sparrow)	Eddie Money; Outlaws; .38 Special; Robbie Dupree
Daniel Amos (NewPax, Alarma, Refuge, Frontline)	XTC; Talking Heads; Beatles; ELO
Daniel Band (Lamb & Lion, Refuge)	Rush; Triumph; Quiet Riot; Crocus
David & the Giants (Myrrh)	Andy Taylor; Glass Tiger; Hall & Oates
DeGarmo & Key (Lamb & Lion, Power)	Doobie Bros.; Bryan Adams; Michael McDonald; Bruce Springsteen; Hall & Oates
Teri DeSario (Dayspring)	Sheena Easton; Barbra Streisand; Christine McVie
Nathan DiGesare (Light)	(Keyboards)
Dion (Dayspring)	
Jessy Dixon (Light, Power)	
DMB Band (Greentree)	Alabama; Oak Ridge Boys; Exile
Linda Dove (Benson)	Debby Boone
D.O.X. (Frontline)	
Phil Driscoll (Sparrow, Benson)	Joe Cocker; Ray Charles; Chuck Mangione; Bob Seger; Herb Alpert
Roby Duke (Good News)	George Benson; Boz Scaggs; Kenny Loggins
Bryan Duncan (Light)	Billy Joel; Orleans; Manhattan Transfer; Hall & Oates
David Eastman (Refuge)	Paul McCartney; Gilbert O'Sullivan; Donald Fagin; Phil Collins; Al Jarreau; Dan Hartman
Chris Eaton (Reunion)	Cliff Richard

Sounds Like...

ARTIST & LABEL	RESEMBLES	CLUB ROCK/DANCE	TECHNO-POP/SYNTH-ROCK	NEW MUSIC/NEW WAVE	HEAVY METAL	HARD ROCK	ROCK	POP ROCK/ADULT CONTEMPORARY	ROCKABILLY/NOSTALGIC ROCK	SOUTHERN ROCK	HEARTLAND ROCK	CLASSICAL ROCK/ORCHESTRAL ROCK	JAZZ/JAZZ FUSION	ISLAND/LATIN/AFRICAN	RAP	SOUL BALLAD	BLUES	SOUL/RHYTHM & BLUES/FUNK	BLACK GOSPEL	COUNTRY ROCK	COUNTRY	FOLK/ROCK	ACOUSTIC	BALLAD	CLASSICAL	PRAISE/HYMNS/TRADITIONAL SACRED	POP/MIDDLE-OF-THE-ROAD	BIG BAND/SWING	INSTRUMENTAL	CONTEMPLATIVE/MEDITATIVE/MOOD
Bertil Edin (Refuge)	Yes; Gino Vanelli; Alan Parsons Project; REO Speedwagon; Phil Collins; Romantics; Al Stewart		★				★	★																						
Edin-Adahl (Refuge)	Asia; Tears for Fears					★	★	★																★			★			
Tony Elenburg (Greentree)	Barry Manilow			★										★																
Elim Hall (Reunion)	Fahrenheit; The Outfield; Police; Sting				★		★	★																						
Joe English (Myrrh, Refuge)	Gino Vanelli; Paul McCartney						★	★																						
Erquiaga, Basel & Nash (Maranatha Colours)	(Guitar)												★												★		★		★	★
Linda Evans (Good News)	Deniece Williams; Marilyn McCoo; Angela Bonfil																	★ ★	★ ★					★		★	★			
Evie (Word)																								★		★				
Farrell & Farrell (Star Song)	Thompson Twins		★					★										★						★		★ ★				
First Call (Dayspring)	Manhattan Transfer; Air Supply							★																★		★ ★	★ ★			
John Fischer (Myrrh)				★				★																						
Followers of Christ (Castle, Onyx)	Stevie Wonder; Jermaine Jackson; Al Jarreau															★		★ ★	★											

Artist (Label)	Compared to
Oden Fong (Frontline)	
4.4.1. (Blue Collar)	U2; Corey Hart; ABC; Spandau Ballet; Duran Duran
Fourth Watch (Exile)	U2; The Alarm; Psychedelic Furs; The Byrds
Don Francisco (NewPax, Myrrh, Star Song)	
Tom Franzak (Myrrh)	Tom Petty; Billy Joel
Rob Frazier (Light)	John Mellencamp
Steve Fry (Sparrow)	
Luke Garrett (Home Sweet Home)	
Jon Gibson (Frontline)	Stevie Wonder; Run-D.M.C.; Aerosmith, Jermaine Jackson
Glad (Greentree)	
Michael Gleason (Kerygma)	Survivor; Genesis
Tanya Goodman (Canaan)	(Synthesizer)
Amy Grant (Myrrh, A&M)	
Keith Green (Sparrow, Pretty Good)	
Steve Green (Sparrow)	
Glen Allen Green (Home Sweet Home)	
Tami Gunden (Home Sweet Home)	Crystal Gayle
Pam Mark Hall (Star Song, Reunion)	Jennifer Warnes; Nicolette Larson; Pat Benatar
Larnelle Harris (Impact, Benson)	
Harvest (Greentree)	
Edwin Hawkins (Birthright, Savoy)	
Tramaine Hawkins (Light, Word)	
Walter Hawkins (Light)	
The Heartbeats (Star Song)	The Go-Go's; Belinda Carlisle
Carel Heinsius Band (Fortress)	

Sounds Like...

ARTIST & LABEL	RESEMBLES	CLUB ROCK/DANCE	TECHNO-POP/SYNTH-ROCK	NEW MUSIC/NEW WAVE	HEAVY METAL	HARD ROCK	ROCK	POP ROCK/ADULT CONTEMPORARY	ROCKABILLY/NOSTALGIC ROCK	SOUTHERN ROCK	HEARTLAND ROCK	CLASSICAL ROCK/ORCHESTRAL ROCK	JAZZ/JAZZ FUSION	ISLAND/LATIN/AFRICAN	RAP	SOUL BALLAD	BLUES	SOUL/RHYTHM & BLUES/FUNK	BLACK GOSPEL	COUNTRY ROCK	COUNTRY	FOLK/FOLK ROCK	ACOUSTIC	BALLAD	CLASSICAL	PRAISE/HYMNS/TRADITIONAL SACRED	POP/MIDDLE-OF-THE-ROAD	BIG BAND/SWING	INSTRUMENTAL	CONTEMPLATIVE/MEDITATIVE/MOOD
Candy Hemphill (Impact, Greentree)																				★				★		★	★			
Kyle Henderson (Kerygma)	Glenn Frey; Men at Work; Police; Bryan Adams; Peter Wolfe					★	★																							
Benny Hester (Myrrh)	Kenny Loggins; Phil Collins; Corey Hart		★				★	★																						
Hadley Hockensmith (Meadowlark)	(Guitars)									★			★	★																
Russ Hollingsworth (Wordsong)																											★			
Dallas Holm (Dayspring)																				★	★			★		★	★			
Nancy Honeytree (Myrrh, Sparrow, Greentree)	Judy Collins; Carly Simon																				★	★	★	★			★			★
Tom Howard Ensemble (Maranatha Colours)	(Ensemble)												★												★				★	★
Larry Howard (Refuge)	Bryan Setzer; Lonnie Mack; Robert Cray																★	★												
Keith Hutchinson (Refuge)	Stanley Clarke; Dave Brubeck; Chick Corea												★															★	★	

Artist (Label)	Comparison
iDEoLA (What?)	Talking Heads; Wang Chung; Rolling Stones; Peter Gabriel; The Kinks
Idle Cure (Frontline)	Glass Tiger; Def Leppard; Steve Perry; Journey; Bon Jovi; Survivor; Night Ranger; REO Speedwagon
Imperials (Dayspring, Myrrh)	
In 3-D (Refuge)	Van Halen; Night Ranger; Billy Squire; Aldo Nova; Foghat; Bad Co.
Jerusalem (Lamb & Lion, Refuge)	Led Zeppelin; Steppenwolf; Golden Earring; Rush; Van Halen
Jeff Johnson (Ark, Meadowlark)	Alan Parsons Project; Pink Floyd
Martyn Joseph (Power)	
Justus (Star Song)	Frozen Ghost; John Mellencamp
Phil Keaggy (Sparrow, Myrrh, Colours)	Paul McCartney; Bruce Cockburn, Steve Morris
Richard Klender (PowerVision)	Sam Harris; Freddie Mercury
Koinonia (Sparrow)	Pat Metheny; Spyro Gyra; Dave Grusin
Brent Lamb (Power)	Paul Young; Kenny Loggins; Jackson Browne
Jeffrey Lams & Kenneth Nash (Maranatha Colours)	(Piano, Percussion)
Mylon LeFevre & Broken Heart (Myrrh)	Gregg Allman; Doobie Brothers
Solveig Leithaug (Dayspring)	
Leviticus (Shadow, Pure Metal)	Armored Saint; Scorpions
Angie Lewis (Power)	
Lifesavers (Frontline)	Modern English; Psychedelic Furs; Depeche Mode; OMD; New Order
Lone Justice (Geffen)	
Look Up (CBS Associated)	Gregg Allman

Sounds Like...

ARTIST & LABEL	RESEMBLES	CLUB ROCK/DANCE	TECHNO-POP/SYNTH-ROCK	NEW MUSIC/NEW WAVE	HEAVY METAL	HARD ROCK	ROCK	POP ROCK/ADULT CONTEMPORARY	ROCKABILLY/NOSTALGIC ROCK	SOUTHERN ROCK	HEARTLAND ROCK	CLASSICAL ROCK/ORCHESTRAL ROCK	JAZZ/JAZZ FUSION	ISLAND/LATIN/AFRICAN	RAP	SOUL BALLAD	BLUES	SOUL/RHYTHM & BLUES/FUNK	BLACK GOSPEL	COUNTRY ROCK	COUNTRY	FOLK/FOLK ROCK	ACOUSTIC	BALLAD	CLASSICAL	PRAISE/HYMNS/TRADITIONAL SACRED	POP/MIDDLE-OF-THE-ROAD	BIG BAND/SWING	INSTRUMENTAL	CONTEMPLATIVE/MEDITATIVE/MOOD
Mad at the World (Frontline)	Depeche Mode; Ultravox; Tears for Fears; Human League; Soft Cell; freeez; New Order		★																											
Phil Madeira (Refuge)																								★						
Darrell Mansfield Band (Polydor, Broken)	Sammy Hagar; .38 Special; Tom Petty						★	★									★													
Marcellino/Navarro (Kerygma)	(Sax, Keyboards)											★	★														★		★	★
Kenny Marks (Myrrh)	John Mellencamp; Bruce Springsteen						★	★			★													★						
David Martin (Home Sweet Home, Greentree)	Paul Davis; Hall & Oates						★	★																						
Debbie McClendon (Light, Star Song)																★		★	★					★		★	★			
Howard McCrary (Good News)																		★	★							★	★			
Phill McHugh (First Vision)	Jack Wagner; Dan Hill																					★		★			★			
David Meece (Myrrh)								★				★												★						
Messiah Prophet (Morada, Pure Metal)	Scorpions; Tesla; Quiet Riot				★																									

Christian Artist	Comparable Artists
Geoff Moore (Power)	Billy Joel; Peter Wolfe; Bryan Adams; Corey Hart; John Mellencamp
Mickey & Becki Moore (Maiden, Milk & Honey)	Peter, Paul & Mary
Ron Moore (Airborn, Morada)	Neil Young; John Mellencamp
Rich Mullins (Reunion)	Bruce Hornsby; Jackson Browne
Michael James Murphy (Milk & Honey)	
Jim Murray (Word)	
New Gaither Vocal Band (Dayspring, Word Nashville)	
Nicholas (Command)	Patti Austin; Marilyn McCoo; Atlantic Starr; Peaches & Herb
911 (Exile)	
Kim Noblitt (First Vision)	The Jets
Larry Norman (Phydeaux, Power)	Leo Sayer; Bob Dylan; The Byrds; Beatles; Rolling Stones
Michael Omartian (Reunion)	(Piano, Synthesizer)
Jamie Owens-Collins (Sparrow, Live Oak)	Linda Ronstadt; Olivia Newton-John; Juice Newton
Twila Paris (Star Song)	Sheena Easton
Leon Patillo (Myrrh)	Sly & The Family Stone; Santana; Earth, Wind & Fire; Lionel Richie
Sandi Patti (Impact, Word)	
Michael Peace (Reunion)	Run-D.M.C.; Kurtis Blow
Charlie Peacock (Exit, Island)	General Public
Dan Peek (Greentree)	America; Beatles
Petra (Star Song, A&M)	Journey; Foreigner; Boston; Bon Jovi; Supertramp; Kansas; Head East

Sounds Like...

ARTIST & LABEL	RESEMBLES	CLUB ROCK/DANCE	TECHNO-POP/SYNTH-ROCK	NEW MUSIC/NEW WAVE	HEAVY METAL	HARD ROCK	ROCK	POP ROCK/ADULT CONTEMPORARY	ROCKABILLY/NOSTALGIC ROCK	SOUTHERN ROCK	HEARTLAND ROCK	CLASSICAL ROCK/ORCHESTRAL ROCK	JAZZ/JAZZ FUSION	ISLAND/LATIN/AFRICAN	RAP	SOUL BALLAD	BLUES	SOUL/RHYTHM & BLUES/FUNK	BLACK GOSPEL	COUNTRY ROCK	COUNTRY	FOLK/FOLK ROCK	ACOUSTIC	BALLAD	CLASSICAL	PRAISE/HYMNS/TRADITIONAL SACRED	POP/MIDDLE-OF-THE-ROAD	BIG BAND/SWING	INSTRUMENTAL	CONTEMPLATIVE/MEDITATIVE/MOOD
Leslie Phillips (Myrrh)	Cyndi Lauper; The Bangles; Stevie Nicks; T-Bone Burnett; Lone Justice	★		★		★	★	★														★		★						
Michele Pillar (Sparrow)	Karla Bonoff; Linda Ronstadt; Carly Simon; Melissa Manchester							★																★			★			
Robyn Pope (Greentree)			★					★																★						
Prism (Reunion)								★																★						
Prodigal (Heartland)	Alan Parsons Project; Journey; Toto; Atlanta Rhythm Section; Michael Sembello							★																★						
Rambo/McGuire (Benson)								★																★			★			
Rap-Sures (Star Song)	Grand Master Mel; Kurtis Blow														★			★												
Rez, Rez Band (Sparrow)	Rainbow; Rush; Jefferson Airplane; AC/DC; Triumph; Iron Maiden; Twisted Sister				★	★																								
Rick Riso (Home Sweet Home)	Al Jarreau; Little River Band; Kool & the Gang; Earth, Wind & Fire; Jermaine Jackson; Sade							★					★	★				★						★						

Artist (Label)	Comparison
Dawn Rodgers (Wordsong)	Judy Collins
Harlan Rogers & Smitty Price (Maranatha Colours)	(Synthesizer)
Scott Roley (Refuge)	
Sacred Fire (Star Song)	
Saint (Pure Metal)	Accept; Ozzy Osbourne; Judas Priest
Phillip Sandifer (Urgent)	Cliff Richard; Harry Chapin
Connie Scott (Sparrow)	Donna Summer; Laura Branigan
2nd Chapter of Acts (Myrrh, Sparrow, Live Oak)	
Servant (Myrrh)	Joan Jett & the Blackhearts; Patti Smyth; Steve Winwood
77's (Exit, Island)	The Byrds; The Kinks; Talking Heads; INXS
Silverwind (Sparrow)	ABBA
Billy Smiley (Meadowlark)	(Horns)
Howard Smith (Light)	James Ingram; Peabo Bryson; George Benson
Michael W. Smith (Reunion)	Duran Duran; Genesis; Mr. Mister; Howard Jones
Paul Smith (Dayspring)	Phil Collins; Earth, Wind & Fire
Richard Souther (Meadowlark)	(Synthesizers)
Billy Sprague (Reunion)	Lou Gramm; Glass Tiger
Candi Staton (Beracah)	
Randy Stonehill (Myrrh)	The Who; The Byrds; Bruce Springsteen; Rick Springfield; Crowded House
Street Angel (Dark)	Velvet Underground; The Call
Stryken (Chrystal)	Motley Crue; KISS

Sounds Like...

ARTIST & LABEL	RESEMBLES	CONTEMPLATIVE/MEDITATIVE/MOOD	INSTRUMENTAL	BIG BAND/SWING	POP/MIDDLE-OF-THE-ROAD	PRAISE/HYMNS/TRADITIONAL SACRED	CLASSICAL	BALLAD	ACOUSTIC	FOLK/FOLK ROCK	COUNTRY	COUNTRY ROCK	BLACK GOSPEL	SOUL/RHYTHM & BLUES/FUNK	BLUES	SOUL BALLAD	RAP	ISLAND/LATIN/AFRICAN	JAZZ/JAZZ FUSION	CLASSICAL ROCK/ORCHESTRAL ROCK	HEARTLAND ROCK	SOUTHERN ROCK	ROCKABILLY/NOSTALGIC ROCK	POP ROCK/ADULT CONTEMPORARY	ROCK	HARD ROCK	HEAVY METAL	NEW MUSIC/NEW WAVE	TECHNO-POP/SYNTH-ROCK	CLUB ROCK/DANCE
Stryper (Enigma)								★																		★	★			
Roy Suthard (Cherry Grove)	Falco																★													
Sweet Comfort Band (Light)	Styx; Raydio; Toto							★																★	★					
Russ Taff (Myrrh)	Michael McDonald; Doobie Brothers; Hall & Oates				★			★											★					★						
John Michael Talbot (Sparrow, Birdwing, Meadowlark)			★			★	★		★	★																				
Terry Talbot (Birdwing, Sparrow)	Neil Diamond; Eagles; Harry Chapin							★												★				★						
Wendy Talbot (Sparrow)	Janis Ian							★		★																				
Steve Taylor (Sparrow)	Devo; Pretenders; Police; Elvis Costello; Psychedelic Furs																							★				★	★	
Terry Scott Taylor (Refuge)	David Bowie; ELO; Beatles; Psychedelic Furs; John Lennon							★																★					★	
Terms of Peace (Patmos)	R.E.M.; Simple Minds; Let's Active; Pink Floyd																								★			★		

Artist	Comparison
Keith Thomas (Dayspring)	Spyro Gyra; Al Jarreau; James Ingram; Freddie Jackson; John Parr; Pat Metheny Group; Jeff Lorber
Kelly Nelon Thompson (Canaan)	
Tonio K. (What?)	Charlie Sexton; Bob Dylan; Cars; T-Bone Burnett
Kathy Troccoli (Reunion)	Kim Wilde; Phyllis Hyman; Miami Sound Machine; Sade
Truth (Benson)	
Twenty Twenty (Power)	Foreigner; Cars; Kansas
Undercover (Blue Collar)	The Clash; B-52s; Police; Berlin; INXS
Vector (Exit, Island)	The Fixx; Echo & the Bunnymen
Greg X. Volz (Myrrh)	
Sheila Walsh (Sparrow, Myrrh)	Sheena Easton; Helen Reddy; Eurhythmics
James Ward (Greentree)	Stephen Bishop; Boz Scaggs
Matthew Ward (Sparrow, Live Oak)	Stevie Wonder
Wayne Watson (Dayspring)	Dan Fogelberg; Boston; Foreigner

Sounds Like...

ARTIST & LABEL	RESEMBLES	CLUB ROCK/DANCE	TECHNO-POP/SYNTH-ROCK	NEW MUSIC/NEW WAVE	HEAVY METAL	HARD ROCK	ROCK	POP ROCK/ADULT CONTEMPORARY	ROCKABILLY/NOSTALGIC ROCK	SOUTHERN ROCK	HEARTLAND ROCK	CLASSICAL ROCK/ORCHESTRAL ROCK	JAZZ/JAZZ FUSION	ISLAND/LATIN/AFRICAN	RAP	SOUL BALLAD	BLUES	SOUL/RHYTHM & BLUES/FUNK	BLACK GOSPEL	COUNTRY ROCK	COUNTRY	FOLK/FOLK ROCK	ACOUSTIC	BALLAD	CLASSICAL	PRAISE/HYMNS/TRADITIONAL SACRED	POP/MIDDLE-OF-THE-ROAD	BIG BAND/SWING	INSTRUMENTAL	CONTEMPLATIVE/MEDITATIVE/MOOD
Wendy & Mary (Birdwing)																						★	★	★						
White Heart (Myrrh, Home Sweet Home, Sparrow)	Toto; Frank Stallone; Robbie Nevil; Journey						★	★																						
Wild Blue Yonder (Frontline)							★	★																						
Fletch Wiley (Star Song)	Chuck Mangione; Tim Weisberg							★					★									★	★		★	★			★	★
Stephen Wiley (Brentwood)	Kurtis Blow														★															
Kelly Willard (Maranatha!)	Crystal Gayle							★																★		★	★			
Deniece Williams (Sparrow)																★		★	★											
Willoughby Wilson Band (Frontline/Calvary)				★																										
BeBe & CeCe Winans (Sparrow, Capitol)	Janet Jackson; Whitney Houston; James Ingram; Freddie Jackson; Jeffrey Osborne															★		★												
The Winans (Light,Qwest)	Jeffrey Osborne; James Ingram																	★	★											
Karla Worley (Star Song)																								★			★			

The Music Comparison Chart is Copyright ©1987 by Paul Baker, P.O. Box 508, Pinson, AL 35126. All rights reserved. Used by permission. **May not be duplicated without written permission from Paul Baker.**

For information on obtaining poster-sized copies of the Music Comparison Chart write to Paul Baker, P.O. Box 508, Pinson, AL 35126.

167